T H E   B O O K   O F

Electric Grilling

T H E B O O K O F

Electric Grilling

LESLEY MACKLEY

HPBooks

HPBooks
A member of Penguin Group (USA) Inc.
375 Hudson Street, New York, New York 10014, USA
Penguin Group (Canada), 10 Alcorn Avenue, Toronto,
Ontario M4V 3B2, Canada (a division of Pearson Penguin
Canada Inc.)
Penguin Books Ltd., 80 Strand, London WC2R 0RL, England
Penguin Group Ireland, 25 St. Stephen's Green, Dublin 2,
Ireland (a division of Penguin Books Ltd.)
Penguin Group (Australia), 250 Camberwell Road,
Camberwell, Victoria 3124, Australia (a division of Pearson
Australia Group Pty. Ltd.)
Penguin Books India Pvt. Ltd., 11 Community Centre,
Panchsheel Park, New Delhi—110 017, India
Penguin Group (NZ), cnr. Airborne and Rosedale Roads,
Albany, Auckland 1310, New Zealand (a division of Pearson
New Zealand Ltd.)
Penguin Books (South Africa) (Pty.) Ltd., 24 Sturdee Avenue,
Rosebank, Johannesburg 2196, South Africa
Penguin Books Ltd., Registered Offices: 80 Strand, London
WC2R 0RL, England

An imprint of **Chrysalis** Books Group plc

Photographer: Philip Wilkins
Home Economist and Stylist: Mandy Phipps
Editor: Katherine Edelston
Designer: Cara Hamilton
Production: Don Campaniello
Filmset and reproduction by: Anorax Imaging Ltd

ISBN: 1-55788-454-4

PRINTING HISTORY
HPBooks trade paperback edition / April 2005

Notice: The information contained in this book is true and
complete to the best of our knowledge. All recommendations
are made without any guarantees on the part of the author or
the publisher. The author and publisher disclaim all liability in
connection with the use of this information.

Printed and bound in China

10   9   8   7   6   5   4   3   2   1

CONTENTS

INTRODUCTION

Grilling is probably the perfect cooking method for any busy lifestyle—a fast, convenient, and healthy way to prepare staple foods such as meat, fish, and vegetables. As we have become increasingly conscious of the need to reduce the amount of fat in our diets, grilling is recognized as a great low fat method, which can be used to cook a wide variety of different ingredients. There is no doubt that in many modern kitchens the oven and frying pan are almost redundant, as grilling becomes the preferred way to cook.

When food, particularly meat, is cooked in the broiler of a home oven, it is not in direct contact with the heat, therefore the heat hits the top of the food first and seals it, while the juices (and therefore nutrients and flavor) drip from the underside into the broiler pan. A ridged contact grill overcomes this by searing and sealing the outside of the food. All the moisture is retained within the food and any excess fat runs off. Grilling in this way has an effect similar to barbecuing; caramelizing the natural sugars on the surface of the food making it look and taste particularly appetizing.

The latest appliance to revolutionize the way we cook our food is the electric grill. This type of grill is growing in popularity as they are compact, easy to use, and are widely available and inexpensive. Described

in simple terms, an electric grill has a hinged lid that closes over the food, searing the outside and sealing in the juices and flavor. Not only that but as both sides of the food are cooked at the same time, the cooking time is considerably reduced and smoke is eliminated.

TYPES OF ELECTRIC GRILL

There is now a wide choice of machines on the market. They come in a variety of sizes and colors and range from basic and functional to those which boast a number of more sophisticated features. The simplest machines consist of a ridged base grill and hinged lid. They have a container for catching the fat; in some machines the grill plate is tilted so that the fat runs off into the container, in others, there are holes in the plate through which the fat can drain away.

A thermostat keeps the grill at a constant temperature, though there can be a tendency for the heat to be greater in the center so it is often necessary to move the food around during the cooking time, to ensure even browning. When the grill is switched on an indicator light will come on. This will go off when the optimum temperature has been

Below: *Electric grills are available in many different shapes and sizes but all are quick and easy to use.*

reached and the grill is ready for cooking. During the cooking time the light will go on and off as a steady temperature is maintained. A useful feature, particularly when cooking larger pieces of meat and poultry, is a variable heat control so that the food can be browned on a higher temperature then the heat reduced to allow the food to be cooked through more slowly. (If the machine you are using doesn't have this feature then you can simply cook thicker pieces of meat in the oven and finish it in the grill.) Some machines have timers, which are another useful addition, particularly when cooking fish, for instance, as the timing can be critical and even an extra minute can make the difference between perfectly cooked and overcooked.

On some models the two halves of the machine can be opened out flat to give twice the surface, for barbecue-style cooking. Electric grills may also have a lid that incorporates a compartment in which bread and buns can be warmed while the meat is cooking. The grill plate on some models is divided in two, with a ridged grill on one side and a flat hotplate, for dry frying eggs and vegetables, on the other. All the machines have a nonstick coating on the grill plates, which makes cleaning easy, but some have removable plates to allow thorough cleaning.

The size of the machine you choose will depend on the number of people you will be cooking for. The smallest are ideal for one or two people while the medium-sized ones are more suited to cooking for a family or for entertaining. Impressive party-sized grills, which can be fitted on a wheeled cart, are perfect for large parties and, with an extension cord, they can be wheeled into the backyard and used like a barbecue, but without all the mess and fuss.

The recipes in this book have been tested on a medium-sized grill, but even so, it is still sometimes necessary to cook food in batches and keep it warm in a low oven until everything is cooked.

COOKING HINTS & TIPS

For best results, anything cooked in an electric grill should be of an even thickness in order to ensure good contact with the grilling surface. The hinged lid adjusts to the thickness of the food, and will accommodate items up to 1 inch thick. Chicken legs and thick pork ribs are not suitable and the ingredients on a kebob skewer should be cut so that they are all roughly the same size.

Cooking times depend on the type of food, its density, and thickness. The cooking times given in this book are simply a guide, as machines vary in power. It is important to check the food during cooking, reorganizing the way it is arranged on the grill, if necessary, and at the end of the cooking time it is essential to check that meat, fish, and poultry are thoroughly cooked through. The instruction book which comes with your grill will give a guide to cooking times for different ingredients, but it is still necessary to check carefully to be sure the food is cooked thoroughly. The table on the right gives the average cooking times for a variety of the most popular foods for grilling.

The most reliable way to check that meat and poultry are cooked properly is by testing it with a meat thermometer or probe, which should be inserted into the center of the meat. The table (bottom right) gives the ideal temperatures to aim for when cooking meat and poultry.

If you do not have a meat thermometer, the following test will give you a reasonably accurate indication of the internal temperature of the meat. Insert a metal skewer into the thickest part of the meat and count to 30. Remove the skewer and carefully touch it on the outside of your wrist. If the skewer is warm the meat is still rare, if it is quite hot, the meat is medium rare, and if the skewer is very hot, the meat is well done. Another way of testing is to pierce the poultry or meat with a fork. If the juices run clear, the meat is cooked. To test whether or not fish is cooked, press it gently and it should feel firm. It will also flake easily when tested with a fork. Raw shrimp will turn pink and feel firm to the touch.

FOOD SUITABLE FOR GRILLING

A wide variety of food is suitable for grilling. The main point to remember is that grilling is a very quick method of cooking, so choose ingredients with that in mind. Meat such as steak, chops, sausages, burgers, and bacon, and poultry such as chicken breasts and thighs, turkey steaks, and burgers are all ideal. Fish also cooks beautifully and grilling will bring out the sweetness in vegetables and caramelizes fruit. Bread toasted on the grill has a delicious charbroiled taste making it perfect for crostini and bruschetta, and toasted sandwiches can be made quickly and easily. Slices of polenta become crisp when grilled. Halloumi cheese, which originates from Cyprus and is a mixture of sheep and goat's cheese, has a mild yet tangy flavor and is perfect for grilling as it keeps its shape and develops a mouthwatering

FOOD	MINS
Beef	
Fillet steak	5–7
Burger $\frac{1}{2}$-inch thick	6–8
Kebobs	7–8
Sausages (thick)	7–8
Pork	
Chops	8–10
Sausages (thick)	8–10
Kebobs	7–8
Ham steak	5–6
Lamb	
Kebobs	7–8
Loin chops	6–7
Poultry	
Chicken breasts	8–10
Chicken/turkey burger	5–7
Chicken/turkey kebob	7–8
Chicken thighs	8–10
Seafood	
Kebobs	5–6
Shrimp	2–3
Salmon fillet	3–4
Tuna steak	5–6
Vegetables	
Asparagus	8–10
Eggplant slices	5
Bell Peppers	8–10
Onions, sliced	10
Fruit	
Pineapple	3–5
Strawberries	1–2
Snacks	
Toast	3–4
Sandwiches	4–5

BEEF	rare	125F	(51C)
and some game	medium	140F	(60C)
	well done	160F	(70C)
CHICKEN & TURKEY		175F	(80C)
DUCK		175F	(80C)
LAMB	rare	125F	(51C)
	medium	140F	(60C)
	well done	160F	(70C)
VEAL		170F	(75C)
PORK	medium	160F	(70C)
	well done	170F	(75C)

flavor. Tofu also grills very success-fully. Other foods ideal for grilling are listed below.

Lamb: chops, kebobs, burgers, steaks
Pork: steaks, kebobs, sausages, burgers, ham steaks, bacon, pancetta
Beef: steaks, burgers, kebobs, sausages
Seafood: fish fillets and steaks, kebobs, scallops, shrimp, fish cakes
Poultry and game: chicken and turkey breasts, chicken thighs and wings, chicken and turkey burgers, chicken and turkey kebobs, venison steaks, burgers, and sausages, duck breasts and kebobs
Vegetables: asparagus, eggplant, zuc-chini, bell peppers, potatoes, fennel, squash, corn on the cob, mushrooms, artichokes, leeks
Fruit: apples, pears, peaches, pineap-ple, mango, bananas, figs, strawberries
Bread: slices of baguette, ciabatta, pannetone, brioche, sandwiches
Others: Polenta, tofu, Halloumi cheese

TIPS FOR GRILLING

• Grilling is a very healthy, low fat way of cooking, but if you are using an ingredient that contains very little fat or none at all, a small amount of oil brushed or sprayed onto the grill

before cooking will prevent the food from drying out. Vegetable, canola, or corn oils are the best for greasing a grill. Apply the oil lightly before heating the grill, either with a brush, pad, paper towel, or oil sprayer. Olive oil tends to smoke so it is better to use it as a marinade ingredient or brushed over food before cooking.

• Always preheat the grill before starting to cook.

• If food is chilled, allow it to reach room temperature before cooking. This will ensure that the food will not burn before it's cooked through.

• Food should be as dry as possible. If using a wet marinade, remove the food from the liquid and pat dry with paper towel.

• Allow the food to seal and develop a crust before attempting to move or turn it, otherwise it may stick.

• As food cooks quickly on grills, it is important to have any accompani-ments and garnishes prepared before you start cooking.

MARINADES & SAUCES

Most food will benefit from being marinated before grilling. There are many advantages to marinating:

• It allows the flavors to penetrate the food, and herbs and spices provide extra flavor.

• The oil in a marinade helps to keep food moist while cooking.

• Vinegar or citrus juice tenderizes meat and game.

• It can be used as a baste.

Marinating is not just for meat or fish, as vegetables can be particularly delicious after being steeped in a herby marinade. Although the recipes in this book stipulate a mari-nating time, food can be marinated for longer or shorter periods to suit your convenience. Fish and seafood does not require lengthy marinating and small cubes of meat or poultry, take less time than larger cuts. Even if you do not have time to leave the

food in the marinade for a few hours or overnight, just a short time will make a difference to the finished dish. Foods that require marinating for no longer than 1 hour can be covered and left at room temperature; otherwise, food should be kept in the refrigerator and allowed to reach room temperature before grilling.

Marinades can be as simple as a splash of lemon oil or seasoned yogurt, or more complicated mixtures of garlic, chili, and other spices. They generally fall into two categories:

Wet Marinades
The ingredients for a wet marinade usually include oil, flavorings, such as fresh herbs and spices, and an acidic liquid, such as citrus juice, vinegar, or wine, or some recipes may contain yogurt. Whatever the ingredients used, food should be marinated in a shallow, nonmetallic dish, such as

Fig.1

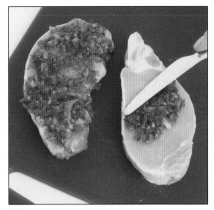

Fig.2

glass or china, which holds the food snugly in a single layer (see Fig.1).

Dry Marinades

A dry marinade, or rub, is a blend of spices and herbs that can be massaged into meat, poultry, or fish. As well as adding an intense flavor, they form a delicious crusty exterior to the food. A marinade made with dry ingredients will keep in an airtight container for several weeks. Before applying a dry marinade, rinse or wipe clean the food and pat dry with paper towels. Lightly oil the food then massage or spread the marinade onto the surface (see Fig.2).

There are a variety of marinades in this book but below are three useful stand-bys. Simply combine the ingredients together and marinate.

Red Wine Marinade:
1 1/4 cups red wine
1/3 cup olive oil
2 cloves garlic, crushed
1 teaspoon dried thyme leaves
1/2 teaspoon dried oregano
1 teaspoon crushed black peppercorns

Sesame Lime Marinade:
2 tablespoons sesame oil
2 tablespoons lime juice
2 tablespoons light soy sauce
1 teaspoon grated fresh ginger
2 teaspoons clover honey

Dry Spice Rub:
2 teaspoons light brown sugar
1 teaspoon sweet paprika
1 teaspoon mustard powder
1 teaspoon ground coriander
1 teaspoon garlic salt
1/2 teaspoon chili powder
1/2 teaspoon dried oregano
1/4 teaspoon ground black pepper

As grilled food is dry and crisp it is always enhanced if served with a sauce or simple salad. There are recipes for sauces, salsas, and salads in this book, but when time is short a squeeze of lemon juice on fish, a spoonful of cooling yogurt with a spicy kebab, or some mayonnaise with shrimp or chicken will make all the difference. Salsas are a cross between a salad and a sauce and are quick and easy to make. A simple tomato salsa consisting of chopped tomato, onion, and chili will give a kick to the simplest dishes and a mango salsa adds a sweet and sour flavor to any Caribbean or Cajun style food.

Herb and garlic butters are easy to make, and they can be prepared well

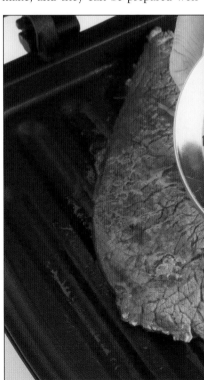

Fig.3

in advance. They can provide a simple yet delicious topping for any char-grilled meat, poultry, fish, or vegetable dish. To make any flavored butter, simply combine 6 tablespoons of softened butter with your preferred flavorings, such as chopped herbs, crushed garlic, or lemon zest and juice. Form the mixture into a log shape (see Fig.3), cover in plastic wrap, and chill until required. To serve, cut into slices and place on top of the hot food or serve on the side with bread.

EQUIPMENT

Grilling is one of the simplest methods of cooking and no special tools or complicated pieces of equip-ment are necessary to achieve deli-cious results. However, there are a few utensils, which will make using the grill even easier.

Grill scraper: this will be supplied with the grill and has indents, which follow the ridges of the grilling plate. It is used to remove any sediment from the grill, before cleaning, and negates the use of harsh, abrasive cleaning products and materials, which will damage the nonstick coating on the grill.

Tongs: these are essential for turning or removing the food from the grill. They should ideally be nylon or plastic to avoid damaging the non-stick coating on the grill plates.

Kebob skewers: these can be metal or bamboo, but remember that the metal ones will heat up, so use oven gloves when removing them.

Meat thermometer or probe: this is an extremely useful device for telling when meat or poultry is thoroughly cooked (see picture below).

Oil spray: these are available already filled, or you can buy the empty sprays and fill with your favorite oil. They are ideal for applying a light film of oil to the food or the grill.

CRABCAKES WITH CHILI MAYO

2 cups fresh crabmeat
2 scallions, chopped
2 teaspoons green Thai curry paste
3/4-inch piece fresh ginger, peeled and grated
1 teaspoon fish sauce
1 tablespoon mayonnaise
1 tablespoon chopped fresh cilantro
3/4 cup white breadcrumbs
all-purpose flour, for dusting
canola oil, for brushing
scallion and fresh chili, to garnish
CHILI MAYONNAISE:
3/4 cup mayonnaise
1 clove garlic, crushed
1 tablespoon Thai sweet chili sauce

To make the crabcakes, mix together the crabmeat, scallions, curry paste, ginger, fish sauce, mayonnaise, and cilantro. Stir in enough of the breadcrumbs to make a firm mixture. Form the mixture into 8 patties and dust with flour. Chill for 1 hour.

To make the mayonnaise, in a bowl, mix together the mayonnaise, garlic, and sweet chili sauce. Set aside. Brush the grill with a little oil. Place the crabcakes in the grill and cook for 5 minutes. Serve with the chili mayonnaise. Garnish with slices of scallion and fresh chili, if desired.

Serves 4

OLIVE & PEPPER BRUSCHETTA

2 yellow bell peppers
2 red bell peppers
3 tablespoons olive oil
salt and freshly ground black pepper to taste
4 slices ciabatta bread
1 clove garlic, crushed
1 tablespoon pesto sauce
8 pitted black olives, roughly chopped, to garnish

Cut the bell peppers into quarters and remove the seeds. Place in a bowl, add 1 tablespoon olive oil, and season with salt and pepper. Toss to coat in the oil.

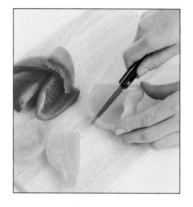

Place the bell peppers in the grill and cook for 10 minutes, until charred and soft, checking and turning from time to time. Remove from the grill and set aside.

Brush the bread slices lightly with olive oil and grill for 4–5 minutes, until toasted. Cut the garlic clove in half and rub over the toasted bread. Spread a little pesto sauce on each slice. Pile the bell peppers on the toast and drizzle with the remaining oil. Scatter the olives over before serving.

Serves 4

EGGPLANT BRUSCHETTA

8 (1/2-inch thick) slices ciabatta
4 tablespoons olive oil, plus extra for drizzling
1 clove garlic
1 tablespoon lemon juice
salt and freshly ground black pepper to taste
1 medium eggplant (long and narrow), cut into
  1/2-inch thick rounds
1 tablespoon chopped fresh mint
5 1/2 oz creamy fresh chevre

Brush the ciabatta with a little oil. Grill for 5 minutes, until browned. Cut the garlic clove in half and rub the cut edge over one side of each piece of ciabatta. Set aside.

In a shallow dish, mix together most of the remaining oil (reserving a little for drizzling), the lemon juice, salt, and pepper. Add the eggplant and turn quickly in the mixture, without allowing it to absorb too much oil. Place the slices in the grill and cook for 5 minutes, until browned and soft.

In a small bowl, mix the mint into the chevre and season with salt and pepper. Spread the cheese mixture over the slices of toast and arrange the eggplant slices on top. Drizzle over the remaining olive oil. Serve at room temperature.

Serves 4

RICOTTA ROULADES

2 medium eggplants (approx. 9 oz each)
3 tablespoons olive oil
9 oz ricotta cheese
3¹/₂ oz soft goat cheese
¹/₄ cup pine nuts, toasted
1 tablespoon chopped fresh basil
salt and freshly ground black pepper to taste
basil leaves, to garnish
TOMATO SAUCE:
1 tablespoon olive oil
1 onion, minced
1 clove garlic, crushed
1 (14-oz) can chopped tomatoes
5 fl oz dry white wine
salt and freshly ground black pepper to taste

To make the tomato sauce, heat the olive oil in a saucepan, add the onion and garlic and cook gently, stirring occasionally, for 10 minutes, until soft. Add the tomatoes, wine, salt, and pepper. Bring to a boil and simmer gently for 20 minutes, stirring occasionally, until thick. Set aside. Cut the eggplants lengthwise, into a total of 18 thin slices, discarding the sides and ends. Brush the slices with oil. Preheat the oven to 375F (190C). Place the eggplant slices in the grill and cook, in batches, for 5 minutes, until brown and soft.

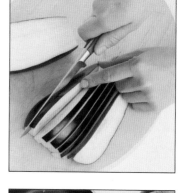

In a bowl, mix together the ricotta, goat cheese, pine nuts, basil, salt, and pepper. Put a spoonful of the filling on one end of each eggplant slice and roll up. Place the rolls, seam side down, in an ovenproof dish. Bake in the oven for 10–15 minutes, until heated through. Reheat the tomato sauce. Divide the sauce among warmed serving plates, arrange the roulades on top, and garnish with basil leaves.

Serves 6

QUESADILLAS

2 cups grated mild cheddar or Monterey Jack cheese
4 flour tortillas
1 fresh red chili
2 scallions
2 tablespoons chopped fresh cilantro
canola oil, for brushing
radishes or cilantro leaves, to garnish

Place a quarter of the cheese in the center of each tortilla.

Halve the chili lengthwise and remove the seeds. Mince the chili, wearing rubber gloves. Scatter the chopped chili over the cheese. Roughly chop the scallions and divide among the four tortillas. Scatter over the cilantro.

Fold two sides of each tortilla into the middle, overlapping, then fold over the ends, to form square parcels. Brush the parcels with oil and place in the grill. Cook for 3 minutes, until toasted and the cheese has melted. Serve, garnished with some radishes or a few cilantro leaves.

Serves 4

— HALLOUMI & SALSA VERDE —

12 oz Halloumi cheese
olive oil, for brushing
SALSA VERDE
3 tablespoons roughly chopped fresh cilantro
3 tablespoons roughly chopped fresh basil
1 clove garlic, minced
1 teaspoon Dijon mustard
3 anchovy fillets
1 tablespoon capers
6 tablespoons olive oil
juice of 1/2 lemon
salt and freshly ground black pepper to taste

To make the salsa verde, place the cilantro, basil, garlic, mustard, anchovies, capers, olive oil, lemon juice, salt, and pepper in a blender or food processor and process until combined, but not completely smooth. Set aside. Cut the Halloumi cheese into 8 slices and brush with olive oil.

Place the cheese in the grill and cook for 4–5 minutes, until golden brown. Serve the Halloumi on warmed plates, with the salsa verde spooned over.

Serves 4

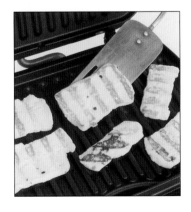

SMOKY EGGPLANT DIP

2 small/medium eggplant
1 clove garlic, crushed
1/2 teaspoon ground cumin
2 tablespoons tahini paste
juice of 1/2 lemon
salt and freshly ground black pepper to taste
2 tablespoons chopped fresh cilantro
1 tablespoon olive oil
SPICED FLATBREAD:
4 pita breads
4 tablespoons olive oil
4 teaspoons coriander seeds, crushed
2 teaspoons dried thyme

Split the pita breads and open out. Brush the cut sides with olive oil and sprinkle with crushed coriander seeds and thyme. Grill for 2 minutes until golden brown and crisp. When cool, break into rough pieces and set aside. Cut the eggplants lengthwise into 4 thick slices and brush with a little olive oil. Grill for 10 minutes, until the skin is blackened and blistered and the flesh is soft. Allow to cool then remove the skin.

Chop the eggplant flesh roughly and place in a colander. Squeeze out as much liquid as possible then place in a food processor with the garlic, cumin, tahini paste, lemon juice, salt, pepper, and cilantro. Process until smooth. Spoon the mixture into a bowl, drizzle with the olive oil, and serve with the flatbread.

Serves 6

PATATAS BRAVAS

1 lb 2 oz medium new potatoes
3 tablespoons olive oil
1 clove garlic, crushed
1 teaspoon smoked paprika (picante pimenton)
salt, to taste
AIOLI:
²/₃ cup mayonnaise
2 cloves garlic, crushed
2 teaspoons lemon juice

To make the aioli, place the mayonnaise, garlic, and lemon juice in a bowl and mix together. Chill until required.

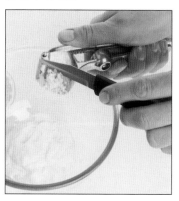

Cook the potatoes in boiling salted water for 15–20 minutes, until tender. Drain thoroughly and leave to cool.

In a large bowl, whisk together the olive oil, garlic, paprika, and salt. Cut the potatoes into ¹/₂-inch thick slices and turn gently in the oil to coat thoroughly. Place the potato slices in the grill and cook for 5 minutes, until browned. Serve with the aioli.

Serves 4–6 as a tapas

— POLENTA & BLUE CHEESE —

3¹/₂ oz Gorgonzola cheese
lettuce leaves, to serve
POLENTA:
4¹/₂ cups hot vegetable broth
7 oz coarse polenta cornmeal
2 tablespoons butter
²/₃ cup grated Parmesan cheese
1 teaspoon finely chopped fresh sage
salt and freshly ground black pepper to taste
olive oil, for grilling

Bring the broth to a boil in a large pan and
slowly stir in the polenta cornmeal. Cook
over a medium heat for about 10 minutes,
stirring, until thick and less grainy. Stir in
the butter, Parmesan, and sage and season
with salt and pepper. Turn the mixture out
onto a flat greased surface and spread into a
rectangle about ¹/₂ inch thick. Smooth the
top and cool until set.

Cut the polenta into 8 pieces. Brush with a
little oil and place in the grill. Cook for
about 5 minutes, until golden. Cut the
cheese into thin slices and place on the
polenta. Serve as the cheese starts to melt,
garnished with lettuce leaves.

Serves 4

GRILLED ASPARAGUS

20 asparagus spears
2 tablespoons olive oil
1 teaspoon white wine vinegar
4 very fresh large eggs
¹/₂ cup Parmesan cheese, shaved
salt and freshly ground black pepper to taste

To trim the asparagus, snap off the woody part at the base of the stems. Brush with some of the olive oil.

Place in the grill and cook for 10 minutes or until tender, depending on the thickness of the spears. Meanwhile, poach the eggs. Bring a large shallow pan of salted water to a boil. Reduce to a simmer and add the vinegar. Break an egg into a saucer and slide the egg into the water. Repeat with the remaining eggs. Reduce the heat until the water is barely simmering and cook the eggs gently for 3–4 minutes, until the whites are set.

Divide the asparagus among 4 heated plates and drizzle with the remaining oil. Remove the eggs with a slotted spoon and place one on each pile of asparagus. Scatter over the shaved Parmesan and grind some black pepper over the top.

Serves 4

LEEK & STILTON POTATO CAKES

7 medium russet potatoes, halved or quartered
1 tablespoon canola oil, plus extra for brushing
1 medium leek
²/₃ cup all-purpose flour, plus extra for dusting
1 large egg yolk
1 cup Stilton cheese, crumbled
salt and freshly ground black pepper to taste
8 slices pancetta

Bring a pan of salted water to a boil, add the potatoes, and boil for 20 minutes, until tender. Heat the oil in a skillet, then add the leeks, and fry gently for 5 minutes, until soft.

Drain the potatoes and return to the pan to dry out over a low heat for a minute then mash until smooth. Stir in the flour, egg yolk, and leeks, season with salt and pepper then leave to cool slightly. Stir the cheese into the mash and mix well. Shape into 8 patties, with floured hands. Chill for 1 hour.

Brush the grill lightly with oil and grill the patties for 5 minutes, until browned and cooked through. Remove and keep warm. Place the pancetta in the grill and cook for 2 minutes then turn and cook for a further minute, until crisp. Serve with 2 slices of pancetta placed on top of each pattie.

Serves 4

PEPPERED GOAT CHEESE

3 ¼-inch log chevre cheese
1 ½ tablespoons coarsely ground black pepper
8 slices French baguette
1 clove garlic, halved
4 cups mixed lettuce leaves
DRESSING:
1 tablespoon balsamic vinegar
¼ cup olive oil
salt and freshly ground black pepper to taste

To make the dressing, put the vinegar, olive oil, salt, and pepper in a bowl and whisk together. Set aside.

Cut the cheese into 6 slices and press the pepper onto all sides of the cheese. Place the baguette slices in the grill and cook for 4–5 minutes, until toasted. Set aside. Place the slices of cheese in the grill and cook for 2 minutes, until lightly browned and beginning to soften.

Place the lettuce leaves in a bowl, pour over the dressing, and toss. Arrange the lettuce on serving plates. Rub garlic onto each slice of toast then place a slice on each plate and top with the cheese.

Serves 6

CROQUE MONSIEUR

4 (¹/₂-inch thick) bread slices from a sandwich loaf
6 tablespoons softened butter
4 slices wafer-thin ham
²/₃ cup grated Gruyere cheese
2 tablespoons grated Parmesan cheese
lettuce leaves, to serve (optional)

Lightly butter the slices of bread on both sides.

Place a thin slice of ham on two of the bread slices. Scatter half of the Gruyere cheese over each slice of ham and then sprinkle the Parmesan on top. Place the second slices of ham on top of the cheese and cover with the remaining slices of bread. Press the sandwiches together firmly then cut off the crusts.

Place the sandwiches in the grill and cook for 4–5 minutes, until the bread is brown and the cheese has melted. Remove the sandwiches from the grill and cut diagonally in half. Serve with lettuce leaves, if liked.

Serves 2

SAVORY GRIDDLED PEARS

2 large dessert pears
2 teaspoons honey
2 cups lambs lettuce
2 cups crumbled Gorgonzola cheese
DRESSING:
1 tablespoon balsamic vinegar
1 tablespoon walnut oil
3 tablespoons olive oil
1 clove garlic, crushed
salt and freshly ground black pepper to taste

To make the dressing, place the vinegar, walnut oil, olive oil, garlic, salt, and pepper in a bowl and whisk together. Set aside.

Cut each pear lengthwise, core, and cut into 4 slices. Brush both sides with a little honey. Place the pears in the grill and cook for 5 minutes, until golden.

Place the lettuce in a bowl, add half the dressing, and toss. Arrange the lettuce on 4 serving plates. Divide the pear slices among the plates and sprinkle over the Gorgonzola cheese. Drizzle the remaining dressing over and serve immediately.

Serves 4

——— GRILLED BELL PEPPER DIP ———

3 red bell peppers
canola oil, for brushing
1 cup walnut pieces
3 cloves garlic, crushed
1 thick slice day-old brown country style bread
juice of 1 lemon
1 teaspoon ground cumin
1–2 teaspoons sweet chili sauce
salt, to taste
$\frac{1}{2}$ cup extra virgin olive oil
pita bread or raw vegetables, to serve

Cut the peppers into quarters and remove the seeds. Brush with oil and place in the grill. Cook, in batches, for 10 minutes, until blackened and soft. Remove from the grill and seal in a plastic bag. Allow the peppers to cool and then remove the skins.

Place the skinned peppers in a blender or food processor. Add the walnuts, garlic, bread, lemon juice, cumin, chili sauce, and salt. Process until smooth then transfer to a serving bowl. Serve with pita bread or vegetables to dip.

Serves 4

HOT & SOUR SOUP

4 scallions, minced
3 teaspoons green Thai curry paste
3 tablespoons chopped fresh cilantro
14 oz ground pork
salt and freshly ground black pepper to taste
canola oil, for brushing
HOT & SOUR SOUP:
6 cups chicken broth
2 lemon grass stalks, cut in half lengthwise
4 kaffir lime leaves
2 slices peeled fresh ginger
3 tablespoons Thai fish sauce
3 tablespoons lime juice
2 cloves garlic, crushed
6 scallions, chopped
1 fresh red chili, seeded and cut into strips
1 bok choy, finely shredded

To make the pork balls, place the scallions, curry paste, cilantro, pork, salt, and pepper in a bowl and mix well. Form the mixture into approximately 24 small balls. Cover and chill for 30 minutes. Once chilled, brush the meatballs with a little oil and place in the grill. Grill for 4–5 minutes, until cooked through.

Place the broth, lemon grass, lime leaves, and ginger in a pan. Bring to a boil then cover and simmer gently for 20 minutes. Strain into a bowl and return the liquid to the pan. Add the fish sauce, lime juice, garlic, scallions, chili, bok choy, and meatballs. Cook for 5 minutes, until heated through then serve in warmed bowls.

Serves 4

PEPPERED SALMON

2 tablespoons mixed peppercorns
pinch of salt
4 (6-oz) salmon fillets
canola oil, for brushing
lemon wedges, to garnish
HERB BUTTER:
6 tablespoons butter
1 tablespoon chopped fresh parsley
1 tablespoon chopped fresh tarragon
1 tablespoon chopped fresh chives
1 tablespoon lemon juice
salt and freshly ground black pepper to taste

To make the herb butter, place the butter in a blender or food processor and process to soften. Add the parsley, tarragon, chives, lemon juice, salt, and pepper and process briefly to combine. Place the butter on a square of plastic wrap and roll into a log shape. Wrap tightly and chill until firm. Allow to soften slightly at room temperature before serving.

Coarsely crush the peppercorns and place on a plate with a pinch of salt. Press the salmon into the pepper. Brush the grill lightly with oil. Grill the salmon for 5–6 minutes, until cooked through. Cut the herb butter into slices and serve with the salmon. Garnish with lemon wedges. Serve with boiled new potatoes and broccoli, if desired.

Serves 4

TUNA SALAD NICOISE

12 oz new potatoes, scraped
1 cup green beans, halved
4 (6-oz) tuna steaks
3 cups mixed lettuce leaves
1 1/2 cups cherry tomatoes, halved
3 large hard-boiled eggs, quartered
8 anchovy fillets in oil, drained
12 black olives
VINAIGRETTE:
1/2 teaspoon Dijon mustard
1 tablespoon white wine vinegar
salt and freshly ground black pepper to taste
1/2 cup extra virgin olive oil
1 tablespoon chopped fresh chives

To make the vinaigrette, whisk together the mustard, vinegar, salt, and pepper. Whisk in the olive oil, then stir in the chives. Set aside. Cut the potatoes in half or quarters, depending on the size. Cook in boiling salted water for 10 minutes, until tender. Drain and return to the pan. Add 1 tablespoon of the vinaigrette, mix gently, and leave to cool. Cook the beans in boiling salted water for 3–4 minutes, until tender but still retaining some "bite." Drain, rinse under cold water, and drain again.

Add the beans to the potatoes and mix together. Brush the tuna steaks on both sides with vinaigrette. Grill for 5–6 minutes, until just cooked through. Place the lettuce leaves in a bowl and toss with half the remaining vinaigrette. Divide the lettuce leaves among 4 serving plates. Arrange the potatoes, beans, tomatoes, eggs, anchovies, and olives on top. Top with the tuna steaks and drizzle over the remaining vinaigrette.

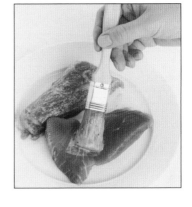

Serves 4

SICILIAN TROUT

1 teaspoon fennel seeds
1 teaspoon dried oregano
1/2 teaspoon cumin seeds
1/2 teaspoon black peppercorns
1/4 teaspoon dried chili flakes
4 (12-oz) trout, cleaned
1/2 teaspoon salt
olive oil, for brushing
2 lemons, quartered and thinly sliced
12 bay leaves
DILL SAUCE:
4 sprigs fresh dill
1/2 cup sour cream
grated zest and juice of 1/2 lemon

To make the sauce, roughly chop the dill. In a bowl mix the sour cream, lemon zest and juice, and dill. Mix well and set aside. In a mortar and pestle, crush together the fennel seeds, oregano, cumin seeds, peppercorns, and chili flakes. Stir in the salt.

Make 3 or 4 cuts on each side of the trout. Brush them with olive oil and rub the spice mixture over the fish, pressing well into the cuts. Push a slice of lemon and a piece of bay leaf into the cuts and brush the fish with a little more oil. Place in the grill and cook for 7–8 minutes, until the flesh flakes when tested with a fork. Serve with the dill sauce.

Serves 4

TERIYAKI TUNA STEAKS

1 tablespoon canola oil
2 tablespoons soy sauce
2 tablespoons rice wine or medium sherry
1 clove garlic, crushed
2 teaspoons soft brown sugar
1-inch cube fresh ginger, peeled
4 (7-oz) tuna steaks
SAFFRON MAYONNAISE:
²/₃ cup fish broth
6 saffron threads
²/₃ cup mayonnaise
1 teaspoon lemon juice
BOK CHOY:
6 baby bok choy, halved lengthwise
2 tablespoons sesame oil
1 tablespoon sunflower oil
1 fresh red chili, seeded and finely chopped

6 scallions, cut into 1-inch lengths
2 tablespoons soy sauce

Place the oil, soy sauce, rice wine (or sherry), garlic, and sugar in a shallow dish. Grate the ginger onto a plate and squeeze the juice into the marinade. Mix well then add the tuna and turn to coat. Cover and chill for 30 minutes. Meanwhile, make the mayonnaise. Boil the broth in a small pan until reduced to 1 tablespoon. Add the saffron and leave to cool. Add the lemon and mayonnaise, mix well, and set aside.

Bring a pan of salted water to a boil, add the bok choy, and boil for 1 minute then drain and plunge into cold water. Drain and set aside. Remove the tuna from the marinade, pat dry with paper towels. Grill for 5–6 minutes, until just cooked through. Heat the oils in a wok. Add the chili and scallions and stir-fry for 1 minute. Add the bok choy and the soy sauce and cook for 3 minutes. Serve the bok choy with the tuna and pour over the mayonnaise.

Serves 4

CREOLE BLACKENED FISH

4 (6-oz) fish fillets, such as sea bass
4 tablespoons butter, melted
2 limes
canola oil, for brushing
CAJUN SPICE MIX:
1 teaspoon salt
1 teaspoon coarsely ground black pepper
1 teaspoon ground cumin
$^1/_4$ teaspoon cayenne pepper
1 teaspoon paprika
1 teaspoon dried thyme
1 teaspoon dried oregano
1 clove garlic, crushed

To make the spice mix, place the salt, pepper, cumin, cayenne pepper, paprika, thyme, oregano, and garlic in a bowl and mix together. Brush the fish fillets with the melted butter then sprinkle each side evenly with the Cajun spice mixture.

Cut the ends off the limes and slice each one in half. Place the halves in the grill and cook for 3–4 minutes, until browned. Set aside. Brush the grill lightly with oil and grill the fish for 3–4 minutes, until blackened and cooked through. Serve with the grilled lime.

Serves 4

CHILI & LEMON SQUID

2 fresh red chilies
1/2 cup olive oil plus extra for brushing
2 lb 4 oz squid, cleaned
salt and freshly ground black pepper to taste
juice and grated zest of 1 lemon
arugula leaves, to serve

Cut the chilies in half lengthwise and remove the seeds. Mince the flesh and place in a pan with the olive oil. Heat gently until just warm then set aside.

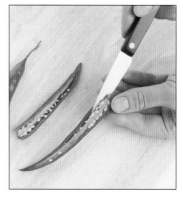

Cut the squid into 2-inch squares and, with a sharp knife, score the outside in a criss-cross pattern, without cutting through the flesh. Brush the squares with oil and season with salt and pepper.

Place in the grill and cook for 3 minutes, checking and turning half way through, if necessary. Meanwhile, whisk together the chili oil and lemon juice and zest. Serve the squid on the arugula leaves with the chili dressing drizzled over.

Serves 4

THAI SPICED SWORDFISH

3 teaspoons Thai green curry paste
grated zest and juice of 1 lime
1 teaspoon fish sauce
2 tablespoons olive oil
4 (6-oz) swordfish steaks
STIR-FRIED GREEN VEGETABLES:
1 tablespoon canola oil
2 cloves garlic, sliced
1-inch piece fresh ginger, peeled and thinly sliced
2 cups small broccoli florets
1 cup snowpeas, trimmed
1 medium green bell pepper, seeded and sliced
4 scallions, sliced
1 tablespoon fish sauce
pinch of sugar
2 cups watercress, trimmed

In a small bowl, mix together the curry paste, lime zest and juice, fish sauce, and olive oil. In a shallow dish add the marinade to the swordfish steaks and turn to coat thoroughly. Cover and chill for 15 minutes. Pat the fish dry on paper towels and place in the grill. Cook for 5–6 minutes, until tender and the fish flakes when tested with a fork.

To prepare the vegetables, heat the oil in a wok or large skillet. Add the garlic and ginger and stir-fry for 1 minute. Add the broccoli florets and stir for 2 minutes, then add the snowpeas and pepper and stir for an additional 2 minutes. Add the scallions, fish sauce, and sugar and stir for an additional 2 minutes then stir in the watercress. Serve with the swordfish.

Serves 4

— MEXICAN SEAFOOD KEBOBS —

1 lb monkfish or other firm fish
12 raw large shrimp, peeled
1 lime, thinly sliced
chopped fresh cilantro, to garnish
4 flour tortillas, to serve (if desired)
MARINADE:
2 tablespoons olive oil
1 tablespoon lime juice
1/4 teaspoon chili powder
1 clove garlic, crushed
2 tablespoons chopped fresh cilantro
CHILI & LIME SAUCE:
4 tomatoes, peeled and seeded
1 tablespoon olive oil
1 fresh red chili, seeded and cut into strips
grated zest and juice of 1 lime

3/4 cup heavy cream
salt and freshly ground black pepper to taste

To make the marinade, place the olive oil, lime juice, chili powder, garlic, and cilantro in a bowl and mix. Cut the monkfish into 1-inch cubes and place in the marinade with the shrimp. Cover and chill for 20 minutes. To make the sauce, cut the tomatoes into 1/2-inch dice. Heat the oil in a pan. Add the chili and cook gently for 1–2 minutes, until soft.

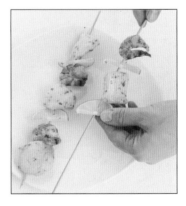

Add the tomato, lime zest and juice, and cook for 2–3 minutes, until soft. Thread the monkfish, shrimp, and lime slices onto skewers. Grill for 5–6 minutes, until cooked through. Stir the cream into the sauce and heat through. Season with salt and pepper. Serve as kebobs garnished with cilantro or remove from the skewers and serve wrapped in tortillas, if liked.

Serves 4

SALMON LINGUINE

2 cloves garlic, unpeeled
1 (8-oz) salmon fillet
canola oil, for brushing
salt and freshly ground black pepper to taste
1 lb 2 oz linguine
1 cup heavy cream
2 cups frozen peas, thawed
2 tablespoons chopped fresh dill

Place the garlic in the grill and cook for 8–10 minutes, until soft. Brush the salmon fillet with oil and season with salt and pepper.

Grill the salmon for 5–6 minutes, until cooked through. Allow to cool then break into large flakes. Set aside. Bring a large pan of salted water to a boil and cook the linguine as directed on the package.

Place the cream and peas in a saucepan. Squeeze the garlic pulp out of its skin, add to the pan, and mix in. Heat gently until warm, add the salmon flakes and dill, then season and warm through. Drain the linguine, reserving 2 tablespoons of the water. Stir the water into the sauce. Toss the pasta into the sauce and serve immediately.

Serves 4

MACKEREL WITH CAPERS

2 cups cherry tomatoes
2 tablespoons olive oil, plus extra for brushing
2 teaspoons capers, rinsed
1 clove garlic, crushed
salt and freshly ground black pepper to taste
1 tablespoon chopped fresh basil
8 (5-oz) fresh skinless mackerel fillets
lemon wedges, to garnish

Cut the tomatoes in half. Heat half of the olive oil in a large skillet and add the tomatoes. Cook for 2–3 minutes, stirring several times, until beginning to soften.

Add the capers and garlic to the tomatoes and season with salt and pepper. Cover and simmer on a low heat for 5 minutes. Stir in the basil and remove from the heat.

Meanwhile, brush the mackerel fillets with the remaining olive oil and season with salt and pepper. Grill for 4–5 minutes, until cooked through. Serve with the tomato and capers. Garnish with lemon wedges.

Serves 4

SCALLOPS WITH ARUGULA PESTO

16 large sea scallops
canola oil, for brushing
salt and freshly ground black pepper to taste
lemon wedges, to garnish
fresh basil leaves, to garnish
ARUGULA PESTO:
3 cups arugula
1/4 cup pine nuts
2 small cloves garlic, crushed
2/3 cup grated Parmesan cheese
juice of 1/2 lemon
1/2 cup olive oil

To make the pesto, put the arugula, pine nuts, garlic, Parmesan, and lemon juice in a food processor or blender. Process until well blended. With the motor running, gradually pour in the olive oil, until thoroughly combined. Season with salt and pepper. Transfer to a serving bowl and set aside.

Pat the scallops dry with paper towels. Brush with a little oil and season with salt and pepper. Grill for 2 minutes, until browned and just cooked through, taking care not to overcook them. Garnish with lemon wedges and basil and serve with the pesto.

Serves 4

CARIBBEAN SHRIMPS

¹/₂ teaspoon hot smoked paprika
¹/₂ teaspoon ground cilantro
1 clove garlic, crushed
juice of ¹/₂ lime
2 tablespoons canola oil
salt and freshly ground black pepper to taste
20 large raw shrimps, in shells, and deveined
MANGO SALSA:
1 mango, peeled and cut into small dice
¹/₂ small red onion, finely chopped
1 fresh red chili, seeded and finely chopped
3 tablespoons chopped fresh cilantro
grated zest and juice of 1 lime
salt and freshly ground black pepper to taste

In a bowl, mix together the paprika, cilantro, garlic, lime juice, oil, salt, and pepper. Add the shrimp and mix to coat thoroughly. Cover and refrigerate for 30 minutes. To make the salsa, place the mango, onion, chili, cilantro, lime juice, salt, and pepper in a bowl and mix together. Set aside.

Remove the shrimp from the marinade and pat dry on paper towels. Thread the shrimp onto skewers and place in the grill. Cook for 4–6 minutes, until pink and firm to the touch. Serve with the mango salsa.

Serves 4

HARISSA CHICKEN

½ cup plain yogurt
2 teaspoons harissa paste
2 teaspoons each ground cumin and coriander
2 cloves garlic, crushed
1 tablespoon olive oil
salt and freshly ground black pepper to taste
4 (6-oz) boneless, skinless chicken breasts
BULGUR WHEAT:
1 cup bulgur wheat
juice of 2 lemons
6 tablespoons olive oil
4 tablespoons chopped fresh parsley
4 tablespoons chopped fresh mint
4 tomatoes, seeded and diced
6 scallions, chopped
salt and freshly ground black pepper to taste

Place the yogurt, harissa, cumin, coriander, garlic, olive oil, salt, and pepper in a bowl and mix together. Place the chicken breasts in a shallow dish and spread the mixture over them. Cover and chill for 2 hours. Meanwhile, cook the bulgur wheat according to the directions on the package, drain well, and transfer to a large bowl. Allow to cool.

Add the lemon juice, olive oil, parsley, mint, tomatoes, and scallions to the bulgur wheat. Season well with salt and pepper. Cover and set aside. Grill the chicken breasts for 8–10 minutes, until cooked through. Serve with the bulgur wheat.

Serves 4

CAJUN CHICKEN

4 tablespoons olive oil
juice of 1 lime
1 teaspoon ground cumin
1 teaspoon ground coriander seed
¹/₄ teaspoon cayenne pepper
1 clove garlic, crushed
1 teaspoon dried thyme
4 (6-oz) boneless, skinless chicken breasts
TOMATO SALSA:
1 lb tomatoes, peeled
1 small red onion, finely chopped
2 tablespoons olive oil
1 tablespoon lime juice
1 tablespoon chopped fresh cilantro
salt and freshly ground black pepper to taste

Make the marinade in a nonmetallic dish, mixing together the olive oil, lime juice, cumin, cilantro, cayenne pepper, garlic, and thyme. Cut the chicken into 1-inch wide strips and add to the marinade. Turn to coat thoroughly. Cover and chill for 3–4 hours. To make the salsa, cut the tomatoes into quarters and remove the seeds. Cut the flesh into small dice and place in a bowl. Add the onion, olive oil, lime juice, and cilantro. Season with salt and pepper. Cover and chill.

Remove the chicken from the marinade and pat dry on paper towels. Grill for 5 minutes, until cooked through. Serve with the salsa.

Serves 4

PIRI-PIRI CHICKEN

1 red bell pepper
4 fresh red chilies
6 tablespoons olive oil
juice of 1 lemon
2 cloves garlic, crushed
1 teaspoon salt
2 lb 4 oz chicken thighs, with skin on
SMOKY PAPRIKA MAYONNAISE:
$1/2$ cup mayonnaise
1 clove garlic, crushed
$1/2$ teaspoon smoked paprika (pimenton)

Cut the bell pepper into quarters and remove the seeds. Place in the grill and cook for 10 minutes, until soft.

De-seed and roughly chop the chili. Place in a blender or food processor with the bell pepper. Add the olive oil, lemon juice, garlic, and salt and process to a paste. Pierce each chicken piece in several places with a sharp knife, place in a shallow dish, and pour over the marinade. Turn the chicken pieces to coat thoroughly. Cover the dish and chill overnight.

Meanwhile, place the mayonnaise, garlic, and smoked paprika in a bowl and stir to combine. Cover and chill until required. Remove the chicken from the marinade and pat dry with paper towels and place in the grill. Grill for 10 minutes, until browned and cooked through. Serve with the mayonnaise.

Serves 4

CHICKEN SATAY

1 lb 2 oz skinless, boneless chicken breasts, cut into
¾-inch cubes
MARINADE:
1 lemon grass stalk, minced
1 clove garlic, crushed
1 teaspoon ground cumin
1 teaspoon ground coriander seed
2 tablespoons soy sauce
1 tablespoon canola oil
SATAY SAUCE:
3 tablespoons smooth peanut butter
1 cup cream of coconut
2 tablespoons red Thai curry paste
1 tablespoon fish sauce
1 tablespoon soft light brown sugar

To make the marinade, place the lemon grass, garlic, cumin, coriander, soy sauce, and oil in a dish and mix together. Add the chicken breasts and turn to coat thoroughly. Cover and chill for 3–4 hours or overnight. Remove the chicken from the marinade, pat dry, and thread onto 4 skewers. Grill for 7–8 minutes, until cooked through.

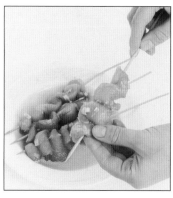

Meanwhile, make the satay sauce. Place the peanut butter, coconut cream, Thai curry paste, fish sauce, and sugar in a pan. Heat gently until smooth and well combined. Add a little water if it is too thick. Serve with the chicken.

Serves 4

—— PESTO-STUFFED CHICKEN ——

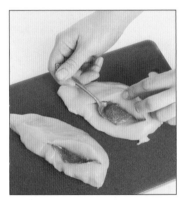

4 (7-oz) skinless, boneless chicken breasts
1 tablespoon pesto
4$\frac{1}{2}$ oz mozzarella cheese
4 bacon slices
TOMATO & AVOCADO SALAD:
2 ripe avocados
6 ripe tomatoes, thinly sliced
6 tablespoons olive oil
2 tablespoons white wine vinegar
pinch of sugar
salt and freshly ground black pepper to taste
1 tablespoon chopped fresh basil leaves

Preheat oven to 350F (180C).

Cut a deep horizontal pocket in the thick side of each chicken breast. Spread a little pesto in each pocket. Slice the mozzarella thinly and stuff the chicken breasts with the cheese. Wrap a slice of bacon round each piece of chicken. Wrap in foil, place on a baking sheet, and cook in the oven for 15 minutes, then remove the foil and transfer to the grill. Grill for 5–6 minutes, until cooked through and golden.

Meanwhile, make the tomato and avocado salad. Halve the avocados, remove the pits, peel, and then cut into slices. Arrange the avocado and tomato on a serving plate. Place the olive oil, wine vinegar, sugar, salt and pepper in a bowl and whisk together. Stir in the basil and spoon the dressing over the salad. Serve the chicken with the tomato salad.

Serves 4

TURKEY ROLL KEBOBS

1 lb 2 oz turkey steaks
3 tablespoons pesto
1 red bell pepper
1 yellow bell pepper
2 small zucchini
1 small red onion
canola oil, for brushing
salt and freshly ground black pepper to taste

Place the turkey steaks between 2 sheets of plastic wrap and beat with a rolling pin until flattened and doubled in size.

Spread the pesto over the turkey and roll up. Cut the red and yellow bell peppers into quarters, remove the seeds, and cut into chunks. Cut the zucchini into $1/2$-inch lengths and cut the onion into eighths.

Cut the turkey rolls into 1-inch lengths. Thread the turkey, peppers, zucchini, and onion onto skewers. Brush with oil and season with salt and pepper. Place the kebobs in the grill and cook for 7–8 minutes, turning if necessary, until browned and cooked through.

Serves 4

— MEXICAN TURKEY STEAKS —

4 (6-oz) turkey steaks
MARINADE:
3 tablespoons olive oil
2 cloves garlic, crushed
1 tablespoon chopped fresh oregano
2 teaspoons ground cumin
1 teaspoon chili paste
juice of 1/2 lime
GUACAMOLE:
2 medium avocados
juice of 1/2 lemon
juice of 1 lime
1 green chili, seeded and minced
1 clove garlic, crushed
pinch of sugar
salt, to taste
2 tomatoes, peeled, seeded, and minced

1/2 small red onion, minced
2 tablespoons chopped fresh cilantro

To make the marinade, place the olive oil, garlic, oregano, cumin, chili paste, and lime juice in a bowl or shallow dish. Add the turkey steaks and turn to coat. Cover and chill for 2 hours. To make the guacamole, cut the avocados in half, remove the stones, scoop out the flesh, and squeeze over lemon juice to prevent browning. Add the lime juice, chili, garlic, sugar, and salt. Mash together to form a rough paste.

Add the tomatoes and stir in the onion and cilantro. Cover closely and chill for 1 hour. Remove the turkey from the marinade and pat dry with paper towels. Place in the grill and cook for 5–6 minutes, until browned and cooked through. Serve with the guacamole.

Serves 4

TURKEY TIKKA KEBOBS

2 tablespoons hot Madras curry paste
4 tablespoons plain yogurt
1 lb 12 oz turkey breast, cut into 1 1/2-inch cubes
MASALA SAUCE:
1 tablespoon canola oil
1 medium yellow onion, minced
2 teaspoons hot Madras curry paste
1-inch piece fresh ginger, peeled and grated
1 (14-oz) can coconut milk
1 cup canned diced tomatoes
2 teaspoons cornstarch mixed with 1 tablespoon
  cold water
salt and sugar, to taste
2 tablespoons chopped fresh cilantro
8 oz easy cook long grain rice, to serve

Put the curry paste and yogurt in a small bowl and mix together. In a separate bowl, add the marinade to the turkey and mix well to coat. Cover and chill for at least 2 hours or, preferably, overnight. To make the masala sauce, heat the oil in a saucepan. Add the onion and cook for 10 minutes, until soft. Stir in the curry paste and ginger. Cook for 1 minute. Put the coconut milk and tomatoes in a blender or food processor and process until smooth. Add to the onion mixture. Stir in the blended cornstarch.

Add salt and sugar. Bring to a boil and simmer for 5 minutes until thickened. Thread the turkey onto skewers and place in the grill. Grill for 7–8 minutes, until browned and cooked through. Remove the turkey from the skewers and add to the sauce. Cook for 5 minutes, then stir in the cilantro. Meanwhile, cook the rice as directed on the package, drain, and serve with the turkey.

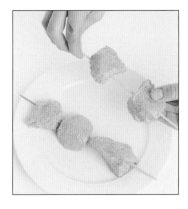

Serves 4

DUCK & MANGO SALAD

2 tablespoons clover honey
1 teaspoon Chinese five spice paste or powder
1 teaspoon soy sauce
2 (6-oz) duck breasts
1¹/₂ cups green beans, trimmed and halved
3 cups mixed salad leaves
1 mango, peeled, pit removed, and thinly sliced
DRESSING:
4 tablespoons canola oil
2 tablespoons sesame oil
1 tablespoon lime juice
1 tablespoon soy sauce
1-inch cube fresh ginger, peeled and grated
2 tablespoons chopped fresh cilantro
freshly ground black pepper to taste

In a bowl, mix together the honey, five spice paste, and soy sauce. Brush all over the duck. Grill for 10 minutes, until cooked through. Leave to rest for 5 minutes. Meanwhile, bring a pan of salted water to a boil, add the beans, and boil for 4 minutes. Drain and refresh with cold water. Set aside.

Place the canola oil, sesame oil, lime juice, soy sauce, ginger, cilantro, and pepper in a bowl and whisk together. Toss the salad leaves with a little dressing and arrange on plates. Place the remaining dressing in a small pan and heat gently. Cut the duck breasts into thin slices and arrange on the salad leaves. Add the mango slices and beans. Drizzle over the warm dressing and serve immediately.

Serves 4

DUCK CAKES WITH PINEAPPLE

4 (7-oz) duck breasts
4 scallions, finely chopped
1 clove garlic, crushed
1 teaspoon finely chopped lemon grass
3/4-inch cube fresh ginger, peeled and grated
1 tablespoon chopped fresh cilantro
1 large egg, beaten
salt and freshly ground black pepper to taste
canola oil, for brushing
PINEAPPLE SALSA:
1 small pineapple
1/2 cucumber, peeled, seeded, and chopped
3 scallions, chopped
juice of 1 lime
1 fresh red chili, seeded and minced
1/4 cup roasted peanuts, coarsely chopped
2 tablespoons chopped fresh cilantro

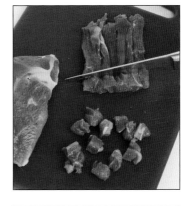

Remove the skin and fat from the duck breasts and cut the flesh into cubes. Place in a food processor and process until minced. Place in a bowl with the scallions, garlic, lemon grass, ginger, cilantro, beaten egg, salt, and pepper. Mix to combine thoroughly. Divide the mixture into six and shape into 3-inch patties. Cover and chill.

Meanwhile, make the salsa. Coarsely chop the peanuts. Trim the pineapple and cut away the skin. Cut into quarters and remove the core. Chop the flesh into small dice and place in a bowl with the cucumber, scallions, lime juice, chili, peanuts, and cilantro. Stir well to combine and transfer to a serving dish. Cover and chill for 30 minutes. Brush the duck patties lightly with oil and grill for 6–8 minutes, until browned and cooked through. Serve with the salsa.

Serves 4

MOROCCAN QUAIL

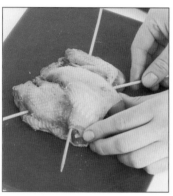

4 quail
3 tablespoons olive oil
juice of 1 lemon
2 cloves garlic, crushed
salt and freshly ground black pepper to taste
2 tablespoons chopped fresh cilantro
SALAD:
1 teaspoon harissa paste
2 tablespoons olive oil
1 tablespoon lemon juice
1 cup cherry tomatoes, halved
$^1/_2$ small cucumber, seeded and cut into cubes
4 scallions, chopped
2 cups watercress

With a pair of kitchen scissors, cut the quail down the backbone, turn them over and press down on the breastbone to flatten them out. Pass 2 skewers through each quail to hold them flat. Place in a shallow dish. In a bowl, mix together the olive oil, lemon juice, garlic, salt, pepper, and cilantro. Pour over the quail and turn to coat with the marinade. Cover and chill overnight.

To make the salad, place the harissa paste, olive oil, lemon juice, salt and pepper in a bowl and whisk together. Add the tomatoes, cucumber, scallions and watercress and toss lightly. Remove the quail from the marinade and pat dry with paper towels. Place in the grill. Cook for 10–15 minutes, until browned and cooked through. Serve with the salad.

Serves 2

CRANBERRY VENISON

4 (7-oz) venison steaks
canola oil, for brushing
salt and freshly ground black pepper to taste
2 teaspoons juniper berries, crushed
GARLIC MASH:
4 cloves garlic, unpeeled
2 lb russet potatoes, peeled
4 tablespoons butter
2–3 tablespoons warm milk
CRANBERRY SAUCE:
1/2 cup red wine
1/2 cup beef broth
1/3 cup cranberry jelly
salt and freshly ground black pepper to taste

To make the mash, place the garlic cloves in the grill and cook for 8–10 minutes, until soft. Cut the potatoes into cubes (1¼-inch) and cook in boiling, salted water for 10–15 minutes, until tender. Drain and return to the pan. Squeeze the garlic pulp out of its skins and add to the potato with the butter and milk. Mash together until smooth. Keep warm. Brush each venison steak with a little oil, rub with salt and pepper and most of the juniper berries, (reserving a little for the sauce).

To make the sauce, put the wine in a saucepan with the broth and remaining juniper berries. Bring to a boil and simmer for 8–10 minutes, until slightly syrupy. Stir in the cranberry jelly and heat gently until melted. Season with salt and pepper. Keep warm. Grill the venison steaks for 4–5 minutes, until browned on the outside, but not too well done in the middle. Serve the steaks with the sauce and garlic mash.

Serves 4

TURKEY BURGERS

1 lb 9 oz ground turkey
1 small onion, minced
1 tablespoon chopped fresh thyme
1 tablespoon chopped fresh parsley
salt and freshly ground black pepper to taste
8 slices pancetta
canola oil, for brushing
CRANBERRY RELISH:
2 tablespoons cranberry jelly
grated zest of $^1/_2$ orange
juice of 1 orange
$^3/_4$-inch piece fresh ginger, peeled and grated
2 tablespoons sugar
1 tablespoon cornflour blended with 1 tablespoon
   cold water

To make the relish, blend the cranberry jelly, orange zest and juice, ginger, sugar, and cornflour mix in a saucepan. Bring to a boil, stir, then cover and simmer gently for 5 minutes until thickened. Transfer to a serving dish and leave to cool.

To make burgers, place the turkey, onion, thyme, parsley, salt, and pepper in a bowl. Mix well to combine. Divide the mixture into four and shape into patties. Wrap 2 slices of pancetta round each one in a cross pattern. Brush the burgers with a little oil and place in the grill. Cook for 6–8 minutes, until cooked through. Serve with the cranberry relish.

Serves 4

— HONEY-MUSTARD CHICKEN —

1 cup pine nuts
2 cloves garlic, crushed
3 tablespoons clover honey
2 tablespoons Dijon mustard
1 tablespoon lemon juice
1 tablespoon soy sauce
2 (7-oz) boneless skinless chicken breasts, cut into
    strips
6 cups lightly packed arugula leaves
DRESSING:
4 tablespoons extra virgin olive oil
1 tablespoon balsamic vinegar
salt and freshly ground black pepper to taste

Put the pine nuts in the grill and cook for 1 minute, until browned. Place the garlic, honey, mustard, lemon juice, and soy sauce in a bowl and mix together. Add the chicken strips to the marinade and toss to coat thoroughly. Cover and chill for 1 hour. To make the dressing, place the olive oil, balsamic vinegar, salt, and pepper in a bowl and whisk together.

Grill the chicken strips for 5 minutes, until cooked through and browned. Place the arugula in a bowl and add enough of the dressing to barely coat the leaves. Arrange a pile of leaves on four plates and stack the chicken strips on top. Sprinkle over the pine nuts before serving.

Serves 4

SPICED GAME HENS

2 cloves garlic, roughly chopped
1 teaspoon ground cumin
1 teaspoon ground coriander
pinch of cayenne pepper
1/2 small onion, chopped
4 tablespoons olive oil
1/2 teaspoon salt
2 Rock Cornish Game Hens
HUMMUS:
1 (14-oz) can chickpeas, drained
4 tablespoons tahini paste
4 tablespoons plain yogurt
2 cloves garlic, crushed
1 tablespoon olive oil
juice of 1/2 lemon

Place the garlic, cumin, coriander, cayenne pepper, onion, olive oil, and salt in a blender or food processor. Process to make a paste. Cut the game hens in half, lengthwise, and place in a shallow dish. Spread the spice paste over the hens. Cover and chill for at least 2 hours or, preferably, overnight.

Meanwhile, make the hummus. Place the chickpeas, tahini paste, yogurt, garlic, olive oil, lemon juice, salt, and pepper in a blender or food processor and process to form a slightly grainy paste. Cover and set aside. Place the hens in the grill and grill for 10–15 minutes, until cooked through and lightly charred. Serve with the hummus.

Serves 4

LAMBURGERS

1 lb lean ground lamb
1 small onion, finely chopped
1 garlic clove, crushed
1 teaspoon ground cumin
1 teaspoon ground coriander seed
1 tablespoon chopped fresh mint
salt and freshly ground black pepper to taste
olive oil, for brushing
pita bread and salad, to serve
TOMATO & OLIVE SALSA:
1 cup mixed pitted olives, chopped
1 small red onion, minced
4 plum tomatoes, peeled and diced
1 fresh red chili, seeded and minced
2 tablespoons olive oil

To make the salsa, put the olives, onion, tomatoes, chili, olive oil, salt, and pepper in a bowl. Mix well, cover, and set aside. In a separate bowl, mix together the lamb, onion, garlic, cumin, coriander seed, mint, salt, and pepper until well combined.

Shape the mixture into 4 burgers and brush with a little oil. Place the burgers in the grill and cook for 5 minutes, until browned and cooked through. To serve, split the pita bread, place some lettuce and tomato on the bottom and then the burgers. Spoon the salsa on top and serve.

Serves 4

LAMB KOFTAS

1 lb 2 oz ground steak
1 small onion, minced
1 clove garlic, crushed
1 tablespoon chopped fresh cilantro
$^{1}/_{2}$ teaspoon ground cumin
pinch of chili powder
salt and freshly ground black pepper to taste
canola oil, for brushing
RAITA:
$^{1}/_{2}$ cucumber
2 teaspoons chopped fresh mint
1 cup plain yogurt
salt and freshly ground black pepper to taste

To make the raita, peel the cucumber, cut in half, lengthwise, and scoop out the seeds. Cut into small dice and place in a bowl. Add the mint, yogurt, salt, and pepper. Stir well and transfer to a serving bowl. Cover and chill. To make the koftas, place the ground steak, onion, garlic, cilantro, cumin, chili powder, salt, and pepper in a bowl and mix to combine thoroughly.

Divide the mixture into 8 and roll into fat hot dog shapes. Press onto 8 skewers and brush with a little oil. Place in the grill and cook for 8 minutes, until browned and cooked through. Serve with the raita.

Serves 4

LEMON BUTTER LAMB

3 tablespoons olive oil
3 tablespoons wholegrain mustard
1 clove garlic, crushed
2 teaspoons ground coriander
salt and freshly ground black pepper to taste
8 (4-oz) lamb loin chops
CHIVE & LEMON BUTTER:
6 tablespoons butter
2 tablespoons chopped fresh chives
1 tablespoon lemon juice
salt and freshly ground black pepper to taste

Place the olive oil, mustard, garlic, ground coriander, salt, and pepper in a shallow dish and whisk together.

Add the chops to the marinade and turn to coat. Cover and chill for 2 hours or overnight. To make the chive and lemon butter, place the butter in a blender or food processor and process to soften. Add the chives, lemon juice, salt, and pepper and process briefly to combine. Place the butter on a square of plastic wrap and mold into a log shape. Wrap tightly with plastic wrap and chill until firm. Allow to soften slightly at room temperature before serving.

Remove the lamb chops from the marinade and place in the grill. Grill for 8–10 minutes, until browned and cooked through. Cut the chive and lemon butter into slices and serve with the lamb chops.

Serves 4

TUNISIAN LAMB BROCHETTES

1 lb lean leg of lamb cut into 1½-inch cubes
8 bay leaves
MARINADE:
4 tablespoons lemon juice
2 tablespoons olive oil
2 cloves garlic, crushed
1 teaspoon ground cinnamon
1 teaspoon ground coriander seed
salt and freshly ground black pepper to taste
ORANGE & RED ONION SALAD:
6 navel oranges
2 small red onions, thinly sliced into rings
1 tablespoon cumin seeds
1 teaspoon coarsely ground black pepper
3 tablespoons chopped fresh mint
6 tablespoons olive oil

salt, to taste
12 pitted black olives (optional)

Place the marinade ingredients in a large
bowl. Add the lamb cubes and mix well.
Cover and chill for 2 hours. Cut the peel off
the oranges, taking care to remove all the
pith. Slice the oranges thinly, reserving any
juice. Arrange the orange and onion slices
in layers in a shallow dish, sprinkling each
layer with cumin seeds, black pepper, mint,
olive oil, and salt. Pour over the reserved
juice and leave for 2 hours.

Remove the lamb from the marinade and
pat dry on paper towels. Divide the cubes
among 4 skewers, adding the bay leaves at
intervals. Grill for 8–10 minutes. Scatter the
olives over the salad (if liked) and serve
with the lamb.

Serves 4

—— BEEF & BELL PEPPER SALAD ——

3 red bell peppers
canola oil, for brushing
1 lb 7 oz sirloin steak
salt and freshly ground black pepper to taste
14 oz new potatoes, cooked
4 cups watercress and baby spinach leaves
2 tablespoons extra virgin olive oil
2 teaspoons lemon juice
HORSERADISH DRESSING:
$^{1}/_{2}$ cup mayonnaise
1–3 tablespoons creamed horseradish
1–2 tablespoons 2% milk

To make the horseradish dressing, place the mayonnaise and horseradish in a bowl and mix together. Add enough milk to thin the mixture to a pouring consistency. Cut the bell peppers into quarters and remove the seeds. Brush with oil and grill for 10 minutes, until soft. Remove from the grill, cut into strips. Set aside. Brush the steak with oil and season with salt and pepper. Grill for 6–8 minutes, until cooked as desired. Leave to cool then cut into slices.

Place the bell peppers in a bowl. Halve the potatoes and add to the bell peppers with the watercress and spinach leaves. In a bowl, mix together the oil, lemon juice, salt, and pepper and pour over the salad. Toss together. Divide the salad among four serving plates. Arrange the steak on top and drizzle over the horseradish dressing.

Serves 4

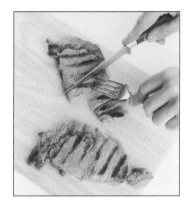

JAMAICAN JERK PORK

1 tablespoon canola oil
2 medium yellow onions, finely chopped
1 clove garlic, crushed
1-inch piece fresh ginger, peeled and grated
1 teaspoon dried thyme
1 teaspoon ground allspice
1 teaspoon ground cinnamon
1 tablespoon hot pepper sauce
2 teaspoons dark brown sugar
juice of 1 large orange
juice and grated zest of 1 lime
salt and freshly ground black pepper to taste
4 (7-oz) pork steaks
grilled butternut squash (page 84), to serve
orange and lime wedges, to garnish

To make the jerk paste, heat the oil in a skillet. Add the onions and cook gently for 10 minutes until soft. Add the garlic, ginger, thyme, allspice, cinnamon, hot pepper sauce, sugar, orange juice, lime zest and juice, and salt and pepper. Simmer for 5–10 minutes, until the mixture forms a dark paste. Leave to cool.

Rub the paste over the pork. Cover and chill overnight. Place in the grill and cook for 6–8 minutes, until cooked through. Serve with grilled squash, garnished with orange and lime wedges.

Serves 4

PORK WITH PEPPERCORN SAUCE

4 (7-oz) boneless pork chops
1 clove garlic, halved
canola oil, for brushing
salt and freshly ground black pepper to taste
GREEN PEPPERCORN SAUCE:
1¼ cups heavy cream
2 teaspoons green peppercorns, drained
1 tablespoon wholegrain Dijon mustard

Trim the excess fat from the chops and rub
the cut garlic clove over both sides. Brush
with a little oil and season with salt and
pepper. Grill for 8–12 minutes, until the
chops are cooked through.

Meanwhile, make the green peppercorn
sauce. Place the heavy cream in a saucepan
and heat gently to warm.

In a mortar and pestle, crush the peppercorns lightly and stir into the sauce with the
mustard, salt, and pepper. Allow the sauce
to bubble a little and thicken. Serve with
the pork chops.

Serves 4

— CARIBBEAN PORK KEBOBS —

1 lb 2 oz lean pork loin, cut into 1¹/₂-inch cubes
3 medium bananas
12 bacon slices
1 red bell pepper, cut into 1¹/₂-inch pieces
1 green bell pepper, cut into 1¹/₂-inch pieces
8 oz easy cook long grain rice, to serve
MARINADE:
1 teaspoon clover honey
1 teaspoon soy sauce
2 cloves garlic, crushed
4 tablespoons pineapple juice
1 tablespoon hot pepper sauce

To make the marinade, place the honey, soy sauce, garlic, pineapple juice, and hot pepper sauce in a bowl and whisk together. Place the pork in a dish and pour the marinade over. Cover and chill for at least 2 hours, turning occasionally. Cut each banana into 4 equal pieces and roll each piece in a slice of bacon.

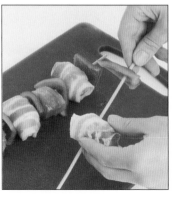

Thread 4 skewers with alternate pieces of red bell pepper, pork, green bell pepper, pork, banana and so on. Place the skewers in the grill and grill for 8–10 minutes, turning once, until the pork is cooked through. Meanwhile, cook the rice as directed on the package and serve with the kebobs.

Serves 4

PORK PATTIES WITH FRITTERS

PATTIES:
1 lb 2 oz pork sausage meat
4 scallions, chopped
2 teaspoons chopped fresh parsley
2 tablespoons ketchup
salt and freshly ground black pepper to taste
all-purpose flour, for dusting
CORN FRITTERS:
1 cup self-rising flour
1 tablespoon chopped fresh chives
2 large eggs
$^1/_2$ cup whole milk
1 (14-oz) can corn, drained
canola oil, for brushing

Place the sausage meat in a bowl and break
up with a fork. Stir in the scallions, parsley,
ketchup, salt, and pepper. Divide the
mixture into eight pieces, roll each piece
into a ball, and then flatten to form patties.
Set aside. To make the corn fritters, sift the
flour into a bowl, add the chives, and season
with salt and pepper. Make a well in the
center. In a bowl, whisk together the eggs
and milk. Gradually whisk the egg mixture
into the dry ingredients to make a smooth
batter. Stir in the corn.

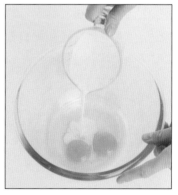

Lightly brush the grill with oil and drop
tablespoons of batter onto the grill and cook
for 2–3 minutes, turning once, until golden.
Keep warm while cooking the patties. Dust
the patties lightly with flour and grill for 5
minutes, until browned and cooked
through. Serve with the fritters.

Serves 4

SAUSAGES WITH PUY LENTILS

2 red bell peppers
4 tablespoons olive oil
salt and freshly ground black pepper to taste
2 medium red onions, sliced
3 cups puy lentils
2 cloves garlic, peeled
1 sprig fresh thyme
8 thick, good quality pork sausages
4 tablespoons chopped fresh Italian parsley

Cut the bell peppers into quarters and remove the seeds. Cut each quarter in half again. Place in a bowl, add 1 tablespoon olive oil, and season with salt and pepper. Toss to coat in the oil. Place the bell pepper pieces in the grill and cook for 8–10 minutes, until charred and soft, checking them and turning from time to time. Remove from the grill and set aside.

Thinly slice the red onions and place in a bowl with half the remaining olive oil. Toss together to coat the onions with oil. Spread the sliced onion in the grill and cook for 8–10 minutes, stirring occasionally, until soft and beginning to caramelize. Remove from the grill and set aside.

When the grill is cool enough, wipe clean with paper towels. Wash and drain the lentils and place in a saucepan. Cover with cold water and add the garlic and thyme. Bring to a boil, cover, and simmer gently for 15–20 minutes, until tender.

Drain the lentils and remove the garlic and thyme. Return to the saucepan. Add the grilled bell peppers and onion and the remaining olive oil. Season with salt and pepper.

Place the sausages in the grill and cook for 7–8 minutes, until browned and cooked through. Reheat the lentils and stir in the parsley. Divide the lentils among 4 warmed plates and place the sausages on top.

Serves 4

— SAUSAGE & POTATO SALAD —

1¹/₂ lb small new potatoes
canola oil, for brushing
8 thin pork breakfast sausages
3 cups baby spinach leaves
SALAD DRESSING:
2 tablespoons extra virgin olive oil
1 teaspoon balsamic vinegar
1 teaspoon Dijon mustard
1 teaspoon chopped fresh rosemary leaves
salt and freshly ground black pepper to taste

Bring a pan of salted water to a boil and cook the potatoes for 10 minutes, until soft. Drain and allow to cool.

Cut the potatoes in half lengthwise and brush with oil. Grill for 6–8 minutes, turning once, until lightly browned. Keep warm. Place the sausages in the grill and grill for 5 minutes, until browned and cooked through.

Meanwhile, to make the salad dressing, add the olive oil, balsamic vinegar, mustard, rosemary, salt, and pepper to a bowl and whisk together. Add to the spinach leaves and toss together. Remove the sausages from the grill and cut into 1-inch lengths. Add to the salad with the potatoes and toss together. Serve immediately.

Serves 4

PANCETTA & PEAR TOAST

1 large pear, such as barlett
8 slices pancetta
FRENCH TOAST:
2 large eggs
5 fl oz full fat milk
salt and freshly ground black pepper to taste
4 (½-inch) thick slices day-old white bread

In a shallow dish, whisk together the eggs, milk, salt, and pepper. One at a time, dip the slices of bread into the egg mixture then turn them over to soak the other side.

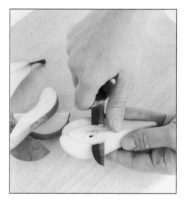

Place the slices in the grill and cook for 4–5 minutes, until golden brown. Keep warm. Cut the pear into quarters, remove the core, and cut into slices. Place the slices in the grill and cook for 2 minutes, until browned and beginning to soften. Keep warm.

Place the slices of pancetta in the grill and cook for 2 minutes, then turn and cook for another minute, until crisp. Serve the toast with the pear and pancetta.

Serves 4

THAI BEEF SALAD

1 lb 2 oz sirloin steak
canola oil, for brushing
salt and freshly ground black pepper to taste
1/2 cucumber
6 scallions
1 red bell pepper
1 tablespoon chopped fresh basil
1 tablespoon chopped fresh cilantro
2 cups iceberg lettuce
1 tablespoon chopped shelled roasted peanuts
DRESSING:
1 tablespoon soy sauce
1 teaspoon clover honey
juice of 2 limes
2 teaspoons sesame oil
1 tablespoon sweet chili sauce

2 cloves garlic, crushed
3/4-inch cube fresh ginger, peeled and grated

To make the dressing, place the soy sauce, honey, lime juice, sesame oil, chili sauce, garlic, and ginger in a bowl and whisk together. Set aside.

Brush the steak with oil and season with salt and pepper. Grill for 5–6 minutes, until cooked as desired.

Allow the beef to cool, then cut into thin slices. Meanwhile, prepare the salad. Peel the cucumber, cut in half, and remove the seeds then cut into matchsticks. Trim the scallions and cut into matchsticks. Cut the pepper into quarters, remove the seeds, and cut into strips.

Place the cucumbers, scallions, pepper, and beef strips in a bowl. Stir in the basil and cilantro.

Pour some of the dressing over the mixture and toss together. Roughly shred the lettuce and arrange on a serving plate. Pile the beef mixture on top. Drizzle with the remaining dressing. Scatter the chopped peanuts over the salad and serve immediately.

Serves 4

STEAK SANDWICH

2 medium red onions
3 tablespoons olive oil
1 ciabatta loaf
2 (4-oz) beef cube steaks
salt and freshly ground black pepper to taste
1 teaspoon finely chopped fresh rosemary
arugula leaves, to serve

Thinly slice the red onions and place in a bowl with half the olive oil. Toss together.

Spread the sliced onions over the bottom of the grill. Cover with the lid and grill for 10 minutes, stirring occasionally, until soft and beginning to caramelize. Remove from the grill and set aside. Wipe the grill clean with paper towels. Cut the loaf in half lengthwise and brush the cut sides with olive oil. Place the two halves in the grill and cook for 3–4 minutes, until warm. Remove, cut in half crosswise, wrap in foil, and keep warm.

Brush the steaks with olive oil and season with salt and pepper. Place in the grill and cook for 4 minutes, until cooked as desired. Scatter arugula leaves over the two bottom halves of the bread. Top with a steak then pile the onions on top. Cover with the remaining bread and serve or leave open, as desired.

Serves 2

SIZZLING STEAK FAJITAS

1 lb 2 oz beef sirloin steak
1 recipe guacamole to serve (page 48)
1 red bell pepper, seeded and cut into strips
1 green bell pepper, seeded and cut into strips
8 flour toritllas
sour cream, to serve
MARINADE:
finely grated zest and juice of 1 lime
2 teaspoons sugar
2 teaspoons dried oregano
1 clove garlic, crushed
$^1\!/_2$ teaspoon chili powder
salt, to taste

To make the marinade, place the lime zest and juice, sugar, oregano, garlic, chili powder, and salt in a shallow dish and mix together. Add the steak and turn to coat in the marinade. Cover and chill for 2 hours. Prepare the guacamole, cover closely, and chill for 1 hour before serving with fajitas. Place the pepper strips in the grill and cook for 5 minutes, until soft. Keep warm.

Pat the steak dry with paper towels and place in the grill. Grill for 6–8 minutes, until cooked as desired. Cut the steak into strips. Warm the tortillas as directed on the packet. Serve the steak and peppers in the tortillas with the guacamole and sour cream.

Makes 8

— BURGERS WITH BLUE CHEESE —

1 medium red onion
1 lb 9 oz ground beef
2 shallots, minced
2 tablespoons Worcestershire sauce
1 clove garlic, crushed
1 tablespoon chopped fresh oregano
salt and freshly ground black pepper to taste
canola oil, for brushing
4 split ciabatta rolls, to serve
1 tablespoon capers
BLUE CHEESE DRESSING:
$^1/_2$ cup mayonnaise
$^2/_3$ cup blue cheese, crumbled
1 clove garlic, crushed
salt and freshly ground black pepper to taste

To make the dressing, place the mayonnaise
in a bowl and stir in the cheese. Add the
garlic and salt and pepper, and mix well
until thoroughly blended. Set aside. Slice
the onion and grill for 5–6 minutes, until
soft and caramelized. Keep warm. In a bowl,
mix together ground beef, shallots,
Worcestershire sauce, garlic, oregano, salt,
and pepper. Divide the mixture into four
and shape into burgers.

Brush the burgers with a little oil and place
in the grill. Grill for 6–8 minutes, until
browned and cooked through. Keep warm.
Wipe the grill with paper towels. Split the
rolls and place in the grill for 1–2 minutes,
until lightly toasted. Place the burgers in the
rolls, and top with the blue cheese dressing.
Serve with the capers and caramelized
onions.

Serves 4

VEGETABLE PITA POCKETS

1 tablespoon pine nuts
4 tablespoons olive oil
2 cloves garlic, crushed
salt and freshly ground black pepper to taste
1 medium zucchini, sliced
1 red bell pepper
1 yellow bell pepper
8 spears baby corn
4 cherry tomatoes, halved
4 pita breads
handful of torn arugula, to serve
8 tablespoons mayonnaise

Place the pine nuts in the grill and grill for 1 minute, stirring twice, until lightly browned. Set aside. In a bowl, mix together the oil and garlic and season with salt and pepper. Cut the zucchini into $^1/_2$-inch slices and place in the dish. Quarter the red and yellow bell peppers, remove the seeds, and cut the quarters in half again. Add to the oil mixture in the bowl along with the baby corn. Toss the vegetables in the oil and place in the grill. Grill for 8–10 minutes, until soft.

Transfer to a clean bowl and add the tomatoes. Split the pita breads to form pockets. Line each pocket with the arugula and spoon 2 tablespoons of mayonnaise into the bottom of each then divide the vegetables among the four pita breads. Scatter the pine nuts over the top.

Serves 4

CHILI POTATO CAKES

1 lb 5 oz potatoes, peeled
1¹/₃ cups cheddar cheese, grated
2 fresh green chilies, seeded and minced
1 clove garlic, crushed
1 large egg, beaten
2 tablespoons chopped fresh cilantro
salt and freshly ground black pepper to taste
all-purpose flour, for shaping
canola oil, for brushing
AVOCADO SALSA:
juice of 1 lime
1 tablespoon olive oil
4 scallions, minced
1 fresh red chili, seeded and minced
2 tablespoons chopped fresh cilantro
salt, to taste
1 ripe medium avocado

To make the salsa, place the lime juice, olive oil, scallions, chili, cilantro, and salt in a bowl and mix together. Cut the avocado in half and remove the pit. Scoop out the flesh and cut into small dice. Stir into the salsa. Cover and set aside. Bring a pan of salted water to a boil. Cut the potatoes into 2-inch cubes, add to the water, and boil for 20 minutes, until tender. Drain the potatoes and return to the pan to dry out over a low heat for 1 minute, then mash until smooth. Allow to cool slightly.

Stir in the cheese, chilies, garlic, egg, cilantro, salt, and pepper. Mix well. With floured hands divide the mixture into eight and shape each piece into a ball then flatten to a patty. Chill for 1 hour. Lightly brush the grill with oil. Place the potato patties in the grill and cook for 5 minutes, until browned and cooked through. Serve with the salsa.

Serves 4

BELL PEPPER PASTA

3 tablespoons finely grated Parmesan cheese
2 tablespoons pine nuts
1 fresh red chili
2 cloves garlic, unpeeled
2 red bell peppers, seeded and cut into eighths
1 lb penne pasta
5 tablespoons olive oil
salt and freshly ground black pepper to taste
3 tablespoons chopped fresh parsley

Sprinkle the Parmesan directly onto the grill to create four equal-size discs. Grill for 1 minute, until crisp (turning half way through if necessary).

Carefully lift the Parmesan crisps off the grill and set aside. Grill the pine nuts for 1 minute, until lightly browned. Set aside. Cut the chili in half lengthwise and remove the seeds. Place in the grill and cook for 3–4 minutes, until soft. Set aside. Place the cloves of garlic and the bell peppers in the grill and cook for 8–10 minutes, until soft. Roughly chop the bell peppers and finely chop the chili. Set aside.

Meanwhile, bring a pan of salted water to a boil and cook the penne as directed on the package. Drain and return to the pan. Stir in the pine nuts, chili, bell peppers, olive oil, salt, and pepper. Squeeze the garlic pulp out of its skin onto the pasta. Stir well to combine and then stir in the parsley. Serve on warmed plates, with a Parmesan crisp on top.

Serves 4

EGGPLANT LINGUINE

1 large eggplant
4 tablespoons olive oil
salt and freshly ground black pepper to taste
1 medium yellow onion, minced
2 cloves garlic, crushed
1 tablespoon capers, drained and roughly chopped
3 tablespoons chopped fresh parsley
1 (14-oz) can diced tomatoes
1 lb linguine
grated Parmesan cheese, to serve

Cut the eggplant, lengthwise, into $1/2$-inch thick slices, discarding the sides. Brush with oil and season with salt and pepper.

Place in the grill and cook for 6–7 minutes, until browned and soft. Set aside until cool enough to handle, then cut into strips. Heat the remaining oil in a skillet. Add the onion and cook gently for 10 minutes, until soft. Add the garlic and capers and cook for 1 minute. Add the parsley, tomatoes, salt, and pepper and simmer for 10 minutes. Carefully stir in the strips of eggplant and remove from the heat.

Bring a pan of salted water to a boil and cook the linguine as directed on the package. Drain well and return to the pan. Add the eggplant mixture and toss well. Serve in warmed pasta bowls with the grated Parmesan scattered over.

Serves 4

VEGETABLE KEBOBS

2 medium zucchini
1 red bell pepper
$^1/_2$ day-old ciabatta loaf
12 button mushrooms
MARINADE:
4 tablespoons olive oil
1 tablespoon balsamic vinegar
1 tablespoon sun-dried tomato paste
1 clove garlic, crushed
1 tablespoon roughly chopped fresh parsley
salt and freshly ground black pepper to taste

Cut the zucchini into $^1/_2$-inch slices. Cut
the pepper in half and remove the seeds.
Cut into 12 even-sized pieces.

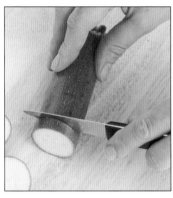

Remove the crusts from the ciabatta loaf
and cut the bread into 1-inch cubes. Thread
the zucchini, bell peppers, bread, and mushrooms onto skewers and place the kebobs in
a large shallow dish.

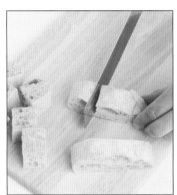

To make the marinade, place the olive oil,
balsamic vinegar, tomato paste, garlic,
parsley, salt, and pepper in a bowl and whisk
together. Brush over the kebobs. Cover and
leave to stand for 1 hour. Place the kebobs
in the grill and cook for 6–8 minutes,
turning once, until browned and the vegetables are soft.

Serves 4

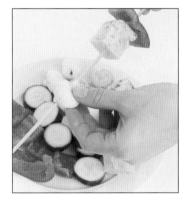

MUSHROOM POLENTA

4 tablespoons butter
2 shallots, minced
1 clove garlic, crushed
2 cups baby bella mushrooms, sliced
2 cups mixed wild mushrooms, sliced
2 teaspoons lemon juice
salt and freshly ground black pepper to taste
4 tablespoons heavy cream
2 tablespoons chopped fresh tarragon
POLENTA:
4¹/2 cups hot vegetable broth
1¹/4 cups coarse polenta cornmeal
2 tablespoons butter
olive oil, for grilling

To make the polenta, place the vegetable broth in a large pan and bring to a boil. Slowly stir in the polenta cormeal and cook over a medium heat, stirring, for about 10 minutes, until thick and less grainy. Stir in the butter. Turn the mixture out onto a flat greased plate and spread into a circle about ¹/2 inch thick. Smooth the top and cool until set. Cut the polenta into 8 wedges. Brush the wedges with a little oil and place in the grill. Grill for 5 minutes, until golden.

Heat the butter in a skillet, add the shallots and garlic and cook for 5 minutes, until soft. Add the mushrooms and cook gently for 2–3 minutes. Stir in the lemon juice, salt, and pepper and cook until the liquid has evaporated. Stir in the heavy cream and tarragon and heat through. Place 2 wedges of polenta on each plate and top with the mushroom mixture.

Serves 4

HALLOUMI STACKS

2 red bell peppers, quartered and seeded
4 tablespoons olive oil
2 medium eggplants
12 oz Halloumi cheese
salt and freshly ground black pepper to taste
TOMATO VINAIGRETTE:
6 cherry tomatoes
2 scallions, finely chopped
6 tablespoons olive oil
1 tablespoon lemon juice
2 teaspoons pesto sauce

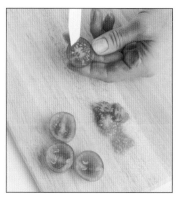

To make the tomato vinaigrette, cut the tomatoes in half and remove the seeds. Cut into small dice.

Place the tomatoes in a bowl with the scallions, olive oil, lemon juice, and pesto sauce and season with salt and pepper. Set aside. Brush the peppers with oil and place in the grill. Cook for 6–8 minutes, until slightly charred and soft. Set aside.

Cut the eggplant and Halloumi cheese into 8 slices each. Brush with oil and season with salt and pepper. Place in the grill and cook for 5 minutes, until browned and soft. Place an eggplant slice in the middle of a serving plate. Lay a slice of Halloumi on top then some red bell pepper. Continue with another slice of halloumi and a slice of eggplant. Repeat on three more plates. Spoon the dressing round the stacks and serve.

Serves 4

KIDNEY BEAN BURGERS

1 tablespoon canola oil
1 medium carrot, minced
1 medium onion, minced
2 cloves garlic, crushed
1 (14-oz) can red kidney beans, drained and rinsed
2 tablespoons chopped fresh parsley
1/2 cup fresh breadcrumbs
1 large egg, beaten
salt and freshly ground black pepper to taste
canola oil, for brushing
4 hamburger buns, to serve
1 sliced tomato, to serve (optional)

Heat the oil in a saucepan. Add the carrot, onion, and garlic and cook for 10 minutes, until soft. Transfer to a bowl and leave to cool. Place the drained beans in a food processor and process until roughly mashed. Add the beans to the onion and carrot with the parsley, breadcrumbs, egg, salt, and pepper. Divide the mixture into four and shape into burgers. Cover and chill for 2 hours.

Brush the burgers with oil and place in the grill. Grill for 6–8 minutes, until browned and cooked through. Keep warm. Split the hamburger buns, place in the grill, and toast lightly for 1 minute. Place the burgers in the buns and serve with the slices of tomato, if desired.

Serves 4

LEEK & GORGONZOLA RISOTTO

6 baby leeks
4 tablespoons olive oil
12 oz risotto rice
²/₃ cup dry white wine
5¹/₂ cups hot vegetable broth
1¹/₃ cups crumbled Gorgonzola cheese
salt and freshly ground black pepper to taste

Trim the leeks and brush with oil. Place in the grill and cook for 10 minutes, until charred and soft. When cool enough to handle, slice into 1-inch pieces with a sharp knife and set aside.

Heat the remaining oil in a large, heavy-based pan, add the rice and stir until coated with oil. Turn up the heat and stir in the wine. Cook, stirring until most of the wine has been absorbed then add 2 ladles of boiling broth. Continue to cook, stirring constantly. Add more broth as the liquid is absorbed.

When all the broth has been added and the rice is tender but still retaining a slight "bite," stir in the cheese and leeks and season with salt and pepper. Allow to stand for 1 minute before serving on warmed plates.

Serves 4

CHILI & LIME SQUASH

1 medium butternut squash
3 tablespoons canola oil
2 teaspoons dried thyme
salt and freshly ground black pepper to taste
CHILI-LIME DRESSING:
²/₃ cup plain yogurt
juice of 1 lime
1 red chili, seeded and minced
2 tablespoons chopped fresh cilantro
salt and freshly ground black pepper to taste

To make the dressing, put the yogurt, lime juice, chili, cilantro, salt, and pepper in a bowl and mix together. Set aside.

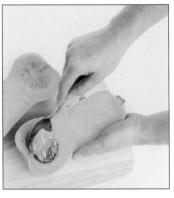

Peel the squash, cut in half, and scoop out the seeds. Cut into ¹/₂-inch thick slices. Mix together the oil, thyme, salt, and pepper and brush over the slices of squash.

Place the squash in the grill and cook for 10 minutes, until browned and soft. Serve with the chili-lime dressing drizzled over or on the side.

Serves 4

ZUCCHINI COUSCOUS

1 1/3 cups couscous
2 cups vegetable stock, boiling
2 medium zucchini, sliced thinly lengthwise
olive oil, for brushing
4 scallions
finely grated zest and juice of 1/4 lemon
2 tablespoons chopped fresh basil
salt and freshly ground black pepper to taste
TO SERVE:
2 teaspoons harissa paste
4 tablespoons olive oil

Place the couscous in a bowl and pour over the boiling vegetable stock, cover with plastic wrap, and leave for 5 minutes, until the liquid has been absorbed. Brush the zucchini slices with oil and place in the grill. Cook for 2 minutes, until browned. Allow to cool. Brush the scallions with oil and place in the grill. Cook for 2 minutes, until beginning to soften. Cut into 1/2-inch slices.

Add the zucchini, scallions, lemon zest and juice, basil, salt, and pepper to the couscous and mix well. To serve, place the couscous in a large serving dish. Place the harissa and olive oil in a bowl and whisk together. Drizzle over the couscous.

Serves 4

HALLOUMI & MUSHROOM KEBOBS

12 oz Halloumi cheese
1 red bell pepper, halved and seeded
1 green bell pepper, halved and seeded
2 small red onions
16 button mushrooms
MARINADE:
juice of ½ lemon
4 tablespoons olive oil
1 clove garlic, crushed
1 tablespoon chopped oregano
salt and freshly ground black pepper to taste

To make the marinade, place the lemon juice, olive oil, garlic, oregano, salt, and pepper in a bowl and whisk together.

Cut the Halloumi cheese and red and green bell peppers into 1-inch squares and cut the onion into quarters. Place in the bowl with the marinade and the mushrooms and stir to coat thoroughly.

Thread the cheese and vegetables onto skewers. Place in the grill and cook for 8–10 minutes, until lightly charred. Serve with bread, if desired.

Serves 4

CHICKPEA & CILANTRO CAKES

2 (14-oz) cans chickpeas
2 cloves garlic, crushed
1 small red onion, minced
2 teaspoons ground cumin
1 fresh green chili, seeded and minced
2 tablespoons chopped fresh cilantro
1 medium egg, beaten
2 tablespoons all-purpose flour, plus extra for
   shaping
salt and freshly ground black pepper to taste
canola oil, for brushing
lemon wedges and green bell pepper slices, to garnish
3/4 cup plain yogurt, to serve (if desired)

Drain the chickpeas thoroughly. Place in a food processor and process until smooth. Add the garlic, onions, and cumin and process until combined. Transfer the mixture to a bowl and stir in the chili, cilantro, egg, and flour. Mix well and season with salt and pepper. If the mixture is too soft add a little more flour. Chill for 30 minutes.

With floured hands, shape the mixture into 12 patties. If time allows, chill again for 1 hour. Brush the grill lightly with oil, place the patties in the grill and cook for 4 minutes, until browned. Garnish with lemon wedges and green bell pepper slices. Serve with plain yogurt, if desired.

Serves 4

— FIGS WITH HONEY YOGURT —

6 fresh figs
3 tablespoons unsalted butter
1 teaspoon ground cinnamon
confectioners' sugar, for dusting
1 tablespoon sliced almonds
HONEY YOGURT:
1 cup plain yogurt
2 tablespoons orange blossom honey
2 teaspoons orange flower water

To make the honey and yogurt, place the yogurt, half the honey, and orange flower water in a bowl and mix together. Set aside.

Cut the figs in half. Place the butter in a small saucepan and heat gently until melted. Stir in the cinnamon. Brush the butter over the figs and dust lightly with confectioners' sugar. Place the figs in the grill and cook for 3–4 minutes, turning once, until warmed through.

Place 2 fig halves on each serving plate. Spoon the yogurt on top, drizzle the remaining honey over, and sprinkle with sliced almonds.

Serves 6

GLAZED PINEAPPLE

1 medium pineapple
confectioners' sugar, for dusting
MINT CREAM:
2 tablespoons fresh mint leaves
1 cup sour cream
2 tablespoons honey

To prepare the mint cream, chop the mint roughly and place in a bowl. Add the cream and honey and stir to combine. Set aside. Cut the ends off the pineapple and remove the skin.

Cut out any "eyes" that remain. Cut the pineapple into 1/2-inch slices, remove the cores, and dust lightly with icing sugar.

Grill for 3–4 minutes, until lightly browned. Serve the pineapple with the mint cream.

Serves 4

SPICED FRUIT KEBOBS

1 small pineapple
2 medium bananas
1 mango
¹/₄ teaspoon freshly grated nutmeg
1 teaspoon ground cinnamon
¹/₂ teaspoon ground ginger
1 tablespoon clover honey
2 tablespoons butter, melted
MAPLE CREAM:
1¹/₄ cups heavy cream
1 tablespoon maple syrup

To make the maple cream, place the cream and maple syrup in a bowl and whip lightly to form soft peaks. Cover and chill.

Peel the pineapple and cut into quarters, lengthwise. Remove the core. Cut into 1-inch cubes. Peel the bananas and cut into 1-inch thick slices. Peel the mango and cut the flesh into 1-inch cubes. Thread the fruit onto skewers.

Put the nutmeg, cinnamon, ginger, honey, and melted butter in a bowl and mix together. Brush the mixture over the kebobs. Place the kebobs in the grill and cook for 5–6 minutes, until warmed through. Serve with the maple cream.

Serves 4

MALLOW MELTS

16 large strawberries (larger than the marshmallows)
16 marshmallows
CHOCOLATE SAUCE:
1/4 cup hazlenuts
4 oz Bournville or any milk chocolate
10 tablespoons light cream
6 marshmallows

Make the chocolate sauce. Place the hazlenuts in the grill and cook for 1 minute, stirring once, until lightly toasted. In a dish-towel, rub the hazlenuts together to remove the skins and finely chop.

Place the chocolate, cream, and marshmallows in a bowl over a saucepan of gently simmering water. Stir continuously, until melted. Whisk until smooth. Stir in the hazlenuts and set aside.

Thread the strawberries and marshmallows onto small skewers and grill for 30 seconds, until just warmed through. Serve with the chocolate sauce drizzled over and sprinkle over the chopped hazlenuts.

Serves 4

PEACH & RED CURRANT DELIGHT

4 ripe peaches
confectioners' sugar, for dusting
RED CURRANT MASCARPONE:
2 cups mascarpone cheese
1 tablespoon confectioners' sugar
2 oz red currants
2 teaspoons caster sugar

To make the red currant mascarpone, place the mascarpone and confectioners' sugar in a bowl and beat together.

Rinse the red currants and place in a small pan. Sprinkle the sugar over and cook for 2–3 minutes over a low heat, until softened. Allow to cool slightly before mixing into the marscapone. Cover and chill until required.

Cut the peaches in half and remove the pits. Dust the fruit lightly with confectioners' sugar and place in the grill. Grill for 3–4 minutes, turning once, until warmed through. Serve the peaches, cut side up, with the mascarpone spooned over.

Serves 4

SUMMER FRUIT FRENCH TOAST

2 cups mixed summer fruit such as black currants,
  blueberries, strawberries, raspberries
³/₄ cup superfine sugar
confectioners' sugar, for sifting
FRENCH TOAST:
2 large eggs
¹/₂ cup 2% milk
3 tablespoons sugar
1 teaspoon vanilla extract
¹/₄ teaspoon ground cinnamon
4 (¹/₂-inch) thick slices day-old brioche loaf

Place the fruit and superfine sugar in a pan
and heat gently until the sugar has dissolved
into the juice. Simmer for 2 minutes.
Remove the pan from the heat and keep
warm. In a shallow dish, whisk together the
eggs, milk, sugar, vanilla, and cinnamon.
Cut the slices of brioche in half, then into
triangles. One at a time, place the brioche
slices in the egg mixture then turn them
over to soak the other side.

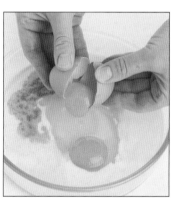

Place the slices in the grill and cook for 4–5
minutes, until golden brown. Serve two
brioche triangles on each plate. Spoon over
the fruit and juice. Dust with powdered
sugar and serve.

Serves 4

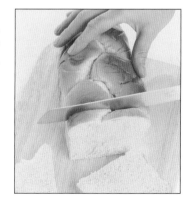

FRUIT CHIMCHANGAS

1 cup raisins
2 tablespoons rum
3 firm bananas
2 tablespoons butter
²/₃ cup soft brown sugar
1 teaspoon ground cinnamon
4 flour tortillas
canola oil, for brushing
confectioners' sugar, for dusting
ice cream, to serve

Place the raisins and rum in a bowl. Leave to soak overnight, until the raisins are plump and the rum has been absorbed.

Cut the bananas into ¹/₂-inch slices. In a skillet, melt the butter. Add the sliced bananas and sugar and stir until the sugar has melted. Mix in the cinnamon and soaked raisins and leave to cool.

Place one quarter of the banana mixture in the center of each tortilla. Fold two sides of each tortilla into the middle, overlapping, then fold over the ends, to form square parcels. Lightly brush the parcels with oil and place in the grill. Cook for 3 minutes until toasted. Dust with confectioners' sugar and serve with ice cream, if desired.

Serves 4

PANETTONE PIECES

5 tablespoons sweet white wine
$\frac{1}{2}$ cup raisins
8 slices panettone
2 teaspoons confectioners' sugar, plus extra for
  dusting
$\frac{1}{2}$ cup ricotta
strawberries, to serve (if desired)

Place the white wine in a small saucepan
and heat until simmering. Add the raisins.
Remove the pan from the heat and let stand
until the raisins have absorbed the wine.

In a bowl, mix together the confectioners'
sugar and ricotta. Spread the mixture over 4
slices of the panettone and scatter the
raisins over the top.

Place the remaining 4 slices of panettone on
top and press down. Sprinkle the sandwiches lightly with confectioners' sugar and
place in the grill. Grill for 3 minutes until
lightly browned. Serve with strawberries, if
desired.

Serves 4

INDEX